OFFICIATING
WRESTLING

A publication for the National Federation of State High School
Associations Officials Education Program

Developed by the
American Sport Education Program

Human Kinetics

Library of Congress Cataloging-in-Publication Data

American Sport Education Program.
    Officiating wrestling / developed by the American Sport Education Program.
        p. cm.
    "A publication for the National Federation of State High School Associations Officials Educa-
tion Program."
    Includes index.
    ISBN: 0-7360-5359-X (soft cover)
    1. Wrestling--Officiating. 2. Wrestling--Rules. I. National Federation of State High School Asso-
ciations. Officials Education Program. II. Title.
    GV1196.27.A44 2005
    796.812--dc22   2004016245

ISBN-10: 0-7360-5359-X
ISBN-13: 978-0-7360-5359-4

The Web addresses cited in this text were current as of September 2005, unless otherwise noted.

NFHS Officials Education Program Coordinator: Mary Struckhoff; **Project Consultant:** Jerry
Diehl; **Project Writer:** Thomas Hanlon; **Acquisitions Editors:** Greg George and Emma Sandberg
Riegert; **Developmental Editor:** Laura Floch; **Assistant Editor:** Mandy Maiden; **Copyeditor:** Alisha
Jeddeloh; **Proofreader:** Erin Cler; **Indexers:** Robert and Cynthia Swanson; **Graphic Designer:**
Andrew Tietz; **Graphic Artist:** Kim McFarland; **Photo Manager:** Dan Wendt; **Cover Designer:** Jack
W. Davis; **Photographer (cover):** Tom Roberts; **Photographer (interior):** Dan Wendt; photos on
pages 1, 6, 9, 15, 18, 21, and 63 © Human Kinetics; photo on page 87 © Sonja Stanbro; **Art Manager:**
Kareema McLendon-Foster; **Illustrator:** Argosy; figure on page 93 reprinted, by permission, from
USA Wrestling, 2003, *International rule book & guide to wrestling* (Colorado Springs, CO: Author);
Printer: United Graphics

We thank Bloomington High School in Bloomington, Illinois, for assistance in providing the location for the photo shoot for this book.

Copies of this book are available at special discounts for bulk purchase for sales promotions,
premiums, fund-raising, or educational use. Special editions or book excerpts can also be created
to specifications. For details, contact the Special Sales Manager at Human Kinetics.

Printed in the United States of America   10   9   8   7   6   5   4   3   2   1

Human Kinetics
Web site: www.HumanKinetics.com

United States: Human Kinetics
P.O. Box 5076
Champaign, IL 61825-5076
800-747-4457
e-mail: humank@hkusa.com

Canada: Human Kinetics
475 Devonshire Road Unit 100
Windsor, ON N8Y 2L5
800-465-7301 (in Canada only)
e-mail: orders@hkcanada.com

Europe: Human Kinetics
107 Bradford Road
Stanningley
Leeds LS28 6AT, United Kingdom
+44 (0) 113 255 5665
e-mail: hk@hkeurope.com

Australia: Human Kinetics
57A Price Avenue
Lower Mitcham, South Australia 5062
08 8277 1555
e-mail: liaw@hkaustralia.com

New Zealand: Human Kinetics
Division of Sports Distributors NZ Ltd.
P.O. Box 300 226 Albany
North Shore City
Auckland
0064 9 448 1207
e-mail: info@humankinetics.co.nz

CONTENTS

PREFACE

It's no secret that officials are an essential part of the sport of wrestling. But how do wrestling officials come to know their stuff? How do they keep all the rules straight? Educational tools and reference materials—such as this book—help officials not only learn their craft but also stay sharp. *Officiating Wrestling* is an invaluable resource for officiating wrestling matches at the high school level. The mechanics in this book have been developed by the National Federation of State High School Associations (NFHS) and are used for high school wrestling throughout the United States.

To get started, you may know a little about wrestling but not much about officiating it. You might know lots about both. The objective of *Officiating Wrestling* is to prepare you to officiate matches regardless of your experience. More specifically, this book will

- introduce you to the culture of officiating wrestling,
- tell you what is expected of wrestling officials,
- explain and illustrate the mechanics of officiating wrestling,
- connect the rules of wrestling with the mechanics of officiating it and
- serve as a reference for you throughout your officiating career.

Officiating Wrestling covers officiating basics, officiating mechanics and specific match situations. In part I, you'll learn who wrestling officials are and what qualities you'll find in a good wrestling official. Part I also differentiates among high school, youth and college officiating and describes match responsibilities. Part II, the meat of the book, describes wrestling mechanics in careful, illustrated detail. Part III highlights some key cases from the *NFHS Wrestling Case Book* and shows how officials apply the rules in action. And finally, part IV provides an introduction to Greco-Roman wrestling and freestyle wrestling for both men and women.

Officiating Wrestling is a practical how-to guide that's approved by the NFHS. This book is also the text for the *NFHS Officiating Wrestling Methods* online course, which has been developed and produced by the American Sport Education Program (ASEP) as part of the NFHS Officials Education Program. To find out how you can register for the online course, visit www.ASEP.com.

NFHS Officials Code of Ethics

Officials at an interscholastic athletic event are participants in the educational development of high school students. As such, they must exercise a high level of self-discipline, independence and responsibility. The purpose of this code is to establish guidelines for ethical standards of conduct for all interscholastic officials.

- Officials shall master both the rules of the sport and the mechanics necessary to enforce the rules, and shall exercise authority in an impartial, firm and controlled manner.
- Officials shall work with each other and their state associations in a constructive and cooperative manner.
- Officials shall uphold the honor and dignity of the profession in all interaction with student-athletes, coaches, athletic directors, school administrators, colleagues and the public.
- Officials shall prepare themselves both physically and mentally, shall dress neatly and appropriately, and shall comport themselves in a manner consistent with the high standards of the profession.
- Officials shall be punctual and professional in the fulfillment of all contractual obligations.
- Officials shall remain mindful that their conduct influences the respect that student-athletes, coaches and the public hold for the profession.
- Officials shall, while enforcing the rules of play, remain aware of the inherent risk of injury that competition poses to student-athletes. When appropriate, they shall inform event management of conditions or situations that appear hazardous.
- Officials shall take reasonable steps to educate themselves about recognizing emergency conditions that might arise during the competition.

PART I

OFFICIATING WRESTLING BASICS

CHAPTER 1

INTRODUCTION TO OFFICIATING WRESTLING

You probably became a wrestling official because you love wrestling. You most likely wrestled at some level and want to remain connected to the sport.

Wrestling has a long, rich tradition. It is the world's oldest sport, with records dating back to the 5th century BCE. It was part of the ancient Olympic Games, which began in 776 BCE, and it was part of the modern Games, which began in 1896.

Officials are part of that tradition, though they are an unobtrusive backdrop to the heroics of the competitors. At the same time, matches can't go on without officials—and as you know, good officiating can make all the difference. Skilled officials allow the wrestlers, coaches and spectators to focus on the efforts of the athletes and the drama of the competition.

Purpose and Philosophy

Your philosophy as an official is the foundation for your approach to your duties. Your philosophy is closely tied to your purpose, which is, in effect, your philosophy carried out. As an official, you have three main purposes:

1. To ensure fair play by knowing and upholding the rules of the sport
2. To minimize risks for the wrestlers to the extent that you can
3. To exercise authority in an impartial, firm and controlled manner, as stated in the NFHS Officials Code of Ethics (see page v)

These three purposes should guide your approach and actions at all times as a wrestling official. Let's take a moment to consider all three.

Ensuring Fair Play

Fair play is at the foundation of all competition. Nothing makes wrestlers, coaches or fans more dissatisfied with competition than if they believe the rules are not being applied correctly and fairly. Competitors expect and deserve officials who know the rules and apply them appropriately in all situations.

Stalling is one of the biggest concerns when it comes to fair play. Recognizing stalling is the key. The *NFHS Wrestling Rules Book* defines stalling this way: Each wrestler must make an honest attempt to stay within the 10-foot (3-meter) circle and wrestle aggressively, regardless of position, time or score, or be called for stalling. This can be a difficult call because it relies on your judgment of the wrestler's intent. You know the rule, but you make the actual call based on your experience and intuition. Conventional wisdom says if you think a wrestler is stalling you are probably late in recognizing it. This is usually the case, so go ahead and make the call. As you gain experience, you will more readily recognize when a wrestler is stalling and be ready to make the call as it happens.

The point is this: To promote fair play, you have to know the rules and you have to enforce them the same way every time. When you do this, you're well on your way to being a good official.

Minimizing Risks

Like all sports, wrestling carries certain risks of injury. In wrestling, the hands and shoulders are particularly vulnerable. The hands are central to holds and much of the action, and shoulders are often unprotected and under stress. The knees and ankles are also vulnerable, especially when the action is fast and wrestlers make many moves and countermoves.

As an official, do all you can to minimize the risks and respond appropriately when a wrestler is injured:

- Know and enforce the rules. Many of the rules were created to minimize injuries.
- Inspect the mat and bench area before all matches and immediately report any illegal or hazardous conditions to event management.
- Maintain authority and control in all aspects.
- Know how to respond to injuries and emergencies.

Exercising Authority

It is vital that you exercise authority in an impartial, firm and controlled manner. You can know the rules backward and forward, but if you can't exercise your authority, you're going to have a difficult time.

Everyone is looking to you to make the correct calls in a manner that doesn't call extra attention to yourself but shows that you know the rules, you know how to apply them fairly and you have control over every situation.

Coaches and players go into most matches respecting the officials and trusting their ability to officiate fairly, but this respect and trust can be lost. If you make calls in an indecisive manner or appear not to know the rules, you are headed for trouble, and it can be difficult to regain authority once you lose it.

To gain and maintain authority, you must know and understand the rules; be firm, decisive, impartial and consistent in your calls; and retain control at all times. When you do this you not only maintain your authority, but you also uphold the honor and dignity of the profession. Coaches and wrestlers prefer officials who know how to exercise the proper authority, in part because this leads to more consistent calls and helps the coaches and athletes know what to expect. Just as wrestlers are expected to prepare themselves to wrestle their best, officials are expected to exercise the appropriate authority in calling the match. This doesn't mean you never miss a call; it means you never lose control of the match.

Who Are Wrestling Officials?

Wrestling officials come from all walks of life—they are teachers, bankers, insurance agents, business executives, factory workers, postal workers and so on. Some wrestled in high school or college, whereas others only participated in youth wrestling. Some are just out of high school while others are retired.

Despite these differences, good officials have much in common. They are critical thinkers who can make decisions in the heat of the moment while remaining calm. They are peacekeepers and negotiators and they know when to step into those roles. They know when and how to stroke an ego without harming the integrity of the sport. They know when and how to sell a call. They have thick skins and an ample amount of patience.

What Makes a Good Wrestling Official?

Like wrestlers, good officials need a range of skills. Sometimes those skills seem almost contradictory. For example, to be a good official, you have to blend into the background yet be omnipresent and authoritative. You have to maintain control yet keep the match in the wrestlers' hands. In the highly emotional arena of sports, you must keep your head about you while all others are losing theirs.

It is inevitable that you will make mistakes; no one is perfect. Learn from your mistakes and do your best never to repeat them.

No one said being a good official was easy. But there are many good officials, and they all got there through dedication to their profession. You can join the ranks of good officials by following the nine prerequisites for good officiating:

1. Know the rules.

To be a competent official you need to know the rules thoroughly. The keys are mastering the rules and enforcing them firmly, consistently and without hesitation.

Thoroughly knowing the rules requires constant analytical study. You will make some decisions over and over, so with experience some calls

Officials must use sound judgment to ensure that the match is executed fairly and safely.

will come by reflex. Prepare yourself to make decisions of every nature through continual study of all possible situations. Eventually fundamentals and correct interpretations will become second nature.

As you study the rules, visualize the situations. These mental images will help you recognize the situations when they occur during matches so you'll be better prepared to make the call. You are not allowed to use television replays or any other equipment to help you make match decisions. Remember, if your calls show that you don't know the rules, you will lose the confidence and respect of wrestlers, coaches and spectators.

2. Know the proper mechanics and positioning.

Your knowledge of the rules might be great, but if your mechanics and positioning are poor, you will have a hard time getting your calls accepted. With proper mechanics, you will always be able to see the action. To be in the right position, you have to constantly be on the move. Try to anticipate the wrestlers' movement and adjust your position to get the best view of the action.

Be particularly alert when wrestlers move near the edge of the mat. Move into position quickly and restart the match when wrestlers go out of bounds. Sometimes you will have to caution the wrestlers to move back to the center of the mat.

3. Experience pressure on the mat.

You need to know when and how wrestlers apply pressure. The best way to gain this knowledge is to spend some time in the wrestling room working with coaches. Get on the mat during clinics to actually *feel* the pressure.

Why is this important? At times, the offensive wrestler must apply pressure to avoid a warning or penalty for stalling. When the offensive wrestler has the opponent broken down and then hooks an arm and maintains pressure on the opponent's shoulder on the mat, it can look like he is applying pressure when he isn't. If you have felt this pressure yourself, you are more likely to interpret the situation correctly.

4. Look sharp and keep fit.

Referees must look like and act like officials at all times. Your physical appearance has a definite effect on the conduct of a match. If you are sloppily dressed, you will find it difficult to keep the match under control. When you are in uniform and you are neat in appearance, you command respect. The proper uniform consists of a short-sleeve knit shirt with alternating one-inch stripes of black and white or an event-provided shirt common to all officials, full-length black trousers, a black belt (if a belt is worn), black socks and black shoes. Other accessories include a red armband on the left wrist, a green armband on the right wrist, a two-colored disk and a black lanyard and black whistle (preferably not a hand whistle). It is imperative that the uniform be clean and well kept. Check your uniform several weeks before the season.

You should have your hair cut in a traditional manner and you should have well-trimmed sideburns. If you have a moustache or beard, keep those trimmed as well. You should also be in good physical condition before the season begins and maintain that level of fitness throughout the entire season.

5. Adopt an appropriate style.

The ideal official notices everything but is seldom noticed. Don't be a showboat; execute your duties without flair. When you take care of your responsibilities with dignity and in conformance with accepted signals and procedures, you encourage wrestlers and spectators to accept your decisions. Being overly dramatic doesn't accomplish anything, and such behavior frequently undermines wrestlers' confidence in your decisions. Quiet dignity is much more effective. Don't be self-important and bossy, but don't tolerate disrespect, either.

Your style can go a long way toward keeping fans off your back. Make your calls in a confident manner, which you develop with experience. With that said, know that you will be heckled. Every crowd includes some fans who believe it's not only their right but their duty to insult the officials. Ignore remarks from the fans. Those same fans who heckle you will lose respect for you if you react to their criticism or show awareness of their heckling. When this happens, their criticism becomes more intense. Good officials turn a deaf ear toward fans and have thick skin that is impervious to barbs and catcalls.

6. Keep safety paramount.

One of your most important responsibilities is to keep the competition as free of risk as possible for the wrestlers. Caution wrestlers who use a potentially dangerous hold and break the hold before it causes injury or becomes illegal. This is where a background as a wrestler helps—you can anticipate potentially troublesome situations and try to prevent them from occurring.

Obviously there is no place for acts that are designed to injure an opponent. Any and all such acts are illegal. Don't hesitate or compromise when these situations occur; enforce the rules to help reduce the risk of injury.

7. Use preventive officiating.

During competition it will often be possible to prevent rule infractions without placing either competitor at a disadvantage. Comments such as "Put down easy," "No higher" or "Work the middle" warn the wrestlers that they are nearing a hazardous situation. This is not coaching; it is making a preventive comment. For example, a wrestler should not move a hammerlock beyond a 90-degree angle. A comment such as "Keep it legal" reminds the wrestler not to move his arm beyond 90 degrees. Often your presence will be enough to discourage an illegal act.

This sort of preventive officiating is desirable; however, you should observe certain limits. For instance, don't talk to wrestlers except when awarding points; issuing warnings, corrections and penalties; or indicating illegal or potentially dangerous holds. To promote action, you might comment, "Center, action and contact." Make sure you direct your comments to both wrestlers, not just one, although of course it is appropriate to remind just one wrestler not to do something illegal.

Another type of preventive officiating consists of stopping potentially dangerous holds before they become illegal or result in injury. While this is not always possible, it is something you should work toward. Here again, your experience as a wrestler is invaluable because you can recognize potentially dangerous holds and move in quickly to stop them.

A courteous, yet professional attitude toward competitors and coaches helps ensure an official's authority.

In general you should avoid touching a wrestler during a match; most wrestlers are taught to stop or release a hold when touched. At times, however, it will be necessary to touch a wrestler to get his attention, particularly when there is a large crowd.

8. Be courteous but don't fraternize.

Be courteous to competitors and coaches but avoid visiting with them immediately before, during or after a match. Never attempt to coach a wrestler, and don't argue with wrestlers, coaches or team representatives. Keep your discussions brief and professional. A dignified attitude often prevents an argument.

Wrestling Official's Tools

There are several tools that can help you excel as an official:

- *The current rules book*. Get it, learn it backward and forward, sleep with it under your pillow—know it as well as you possibly can. Always have your rules book with you when you officiate. It is best to keep it at the scorer's table.
- *Educational resources*. Use this book and the *Officiating Wrestling Mechanics* CD as well as magazines and other resources to hone your skills.
- *First-hand experience*. Use every officiating experience to expand your knowledge of the sport and improve your ability to officiate.
- *Second-hand experience*. Learn from watching other officials, either in person or on video. Watch their mechanics, how they exercise their authority and how they make their calls. Adapt what is useful to your own style.
- *Clinics and workshops*. Attend as many rules clinics as possible. If none are offered in your area, suggest to veteran officials that local referees design a clinic of their own. Speak with the schools in your area and develop a wrestling workshop. And don't stop with one clinic or course; continue to learn throughout your career.
- *Officiating journal*. Keep a journal as a self-assessment tool, charting successes, areas for improvement, progress and things learned from each match.
- *Review from others*. Request a fellow official from your local officials' chapter to come watch you and critique your work.
- *Self-review*. Have a friend videotape a match for you to review or borrow a videotape of one of your matches from a coach.

9. Know your jurisdiction.

Your jurisdiction begins when you arrive at the site of the competition and ends when you approve the scorebook at dual meets or sign the bout card following the last match of a tournament. At dual meets and tournaments you have jurisdiction in the mat area even when you are not working on the mat. The match referee is responsible for the match in progress but other referees can offer assistance to the match referee. Just because you are not working on a particular mat doesn't mean you don't have responsibilities. Anytime you see action that is not observed by the mat referee, communicate with the mat referee as soon as possible.

Officiating at the High School Level

Officiating wrestling at the high school level is similar to officiating at other levels, but in some aspects the high school experience is unique.

You might have officiated at youth levels where the officials sometimes coach the wrestlers during a match, giving them technique tips or allowing them to bend the rules as they learn the sport. At the high school level you neither bend the rules nor coach the wrestlers. You simply call the match fairly and authoritatively.

Another difference is the number of officials. At youth levels you usually have only one official. At the high school level you might be part of a two-referee crew, depending on your state association's rules. When a referee and assistant referee both work a match, they each have the same mobility. While the assistant referee can assist in making calls, the referee is in control of the match and is the only official who can award points or call a fall. See chapter 2 for more on the roles of referee and assistant referee.

The most significant difference between the high school and collegiate levels is that in high school a fall must be held for two seconds, while in college a fall has to be held for only one second. Additionally, high school wrestlers compete in three periods of two minutes each while colleges use a two-minute first period followed by two three-minute periods. Other differences include fleeing the mat and potentially dangerous holds; both are allowed to progress longer at the collegiate level.

As a high school wrestling official, you'll be part of the NFHS Officials Association. Through your state officials' association, you can receive assignments, attend annual rules meetings to learn new rules and attend clinics throughout the year. Take advantage of your membership within the NFHS Officials Association and your state organization to continue to develop your skills.

Now that we've considered the foundation of being a wrestling official, let's take a look at meet responsibilities and procedures, which are the focus of the next chapter.

CHAPTER 2

MEET RESPONSIBILITIES AND PROCEDURES

In the previous chapter we considered the referee's purpose, what makes a good referee and tools for growing in the profession. In this chapter we'll discuss the responsibilities of the referee and assistant referee. There will also be discussion on how to handle specific postmeet duties.

Referee Responsibilities

Your most important premeet duty is weighing in the contestants. To supervise weigh-ins, you should arrive no later than 45 minutes before weigh-ins are scheduled to begin. If you are not able to do so, notify the home school so they can arrange to have the weigh-ins properly supervised. Make sure you plan for the unexpected, such as traffic jams or car problems, and allow yourself ample time to get to the gym. Following is a list of your main premeet duties.

Weigh-Ins

Unless a school has made arrangements for another authorized person to supervise weigh-ins, conducting weigh-ins is your responsibility. You need to confirm the weigh-in schedule, arrive at the appointed time, check the scales, validate each wrestler's weight, record names and check the weight classes. If you are not conducting the weigh-ins, as soon as you get to the gym and change into your officiating clothes report to the authorities who have conducted the weigh-ins.

Inspections

When you are conducting weigh-ins, you need to inspect the wrestlers, uniforms and equipment. If you are not conducting weigh-ins, you

Preseason Duties

Just as you have premeet duties, you have preseason duties.

- *Know the rules.* Study the rules. Join a local officials' organization. Attend rules meetings and clinics. Keep up on changes and interpretations. Work on mechanics and preventive officiating.
- *Take care of your appearance and be in good shape.* Get in and maintain top physical condition. This will help you physically as you officiate meets, and it will help coaches, wrestlers and fans more readily accept your calls. Good grooming also helps you command respect.
- *Work preseason scrimmages.* Working some preseason scrimmages will help prepare you for officiating meets. Contact a local school and offer to work some challenge matches. In addition, many schools have a team night or open house before the first contest. Offer to explain the rules to parents and fans, which could reduce the number of problems you encounter during the season.
- *Verify your officiating schedule.* Make sure all dates and sites are accurate. Consider sending a card to the principal or athletic director of schools where you will be officiating, confirming with them that they are on your schedule.

may do inspections after you arrive at the gym and check in with the authorities who conducted the weigh-ins. Visit the locker rooms and assess the wrestlers for grooming, objectionable padding and communicable diseases. Any wrestler opting to wear a legal hair cover for hair that doesn't satisfy the hair rule must wear it to the weigh-in. Additionally, when you inspect the wrestlers, be sure that a coach is present.

If you suspect a wrestler of having a communicable skin disease or any other condition that makes participation inadvisable, the wrestler's coach must provide written documentation from a physician stating that the suspected condition is not communicable and that the athlete's participation would not be harmful to an opponent. This document shall be furnished at the weigh-in or prior to competition. (Forms can be found on the NFHS Web site, www.NFHS.org.) Each wrestler must comply with standard health, sanitary and safety measures.

You must also be certain that the wrestlers' hair complies with the grooming rule, that fingernails are smooth and clipped short, and that wrestlers are wearing no jewelry of any kind. In addition, make sure

Before the start of the meet the referee must attend to several premeet responsibilities, including ensuring that uniforms and equipment are in accordance with the rules.

that all equipment is legal and any use of protective padding and tape is within the rules. If you are officiating at a tournament, the best time to conduct this inspection is at the weigh-ins or individually at the side of the mat.

Information Review

While making premeet inspections in the locker room, you might want to briefly cover the following topics, if applicable:

- Pertinent rule changes
- Duties of the captains as to the conduct of their team
- Good sporting behavior
- Flip of the disk
- Choice of position
- Starting positions
- Starting and stopping on the whistle
- Injury procedure
- Stalling
- How you will handle out-of-bounds situations

- Your general view of control
- Takedowns (tell the wrestlers they can't defend a lead but must attempt to secure a takedown)
- End-of-match procedures

Some referees also like to inform the wrestlers that as referee, they are assuming the wrestlers are in condition. Stalling calls, therefore, will be made with that in mind. For example, should a wrestler fail to improve his position because of poor conditioning, stalling will be called.

Wrestling Area

Make sure that the mat has the proper markings and all taping is secure. Also check the safety area, the size of the mats, the bench areas and the scorer's table. Make certain that the team bench area is at least 10 feet (3 meters) from the edge of the mat and the scorer's table, if possible.

Proper and Improper Uniforms

One of your duties is to inspect wrestlers and their uniforms before wrestling. Here are some guidelines for uniform inspection.

Wrestlers should wear singlets with full-length tights and stirrups. Their uniforms must be school-issued. Shorter tights and other accessories that extend beyond the inseam of a one-piece uniform are not permitted. Wrestlers must also wear wrestling ear guards and heelless wrestling shoes that reach above the ankles. If shoelaces are visible, they must be secured in an acceptable fashion.

The rules forbid wrestlers from wearing a T-shirt or anything else under the uniform except when you determine there is sufficient reason to do so. For instance, if a wrestler has severe acne on his shoulders or is protecting some other skin condition, you might allow him to wear a tight-fitting, short-sleeved shirt, but it must be of a single solid color, unadorned.

After you have inspected the wrestlers and their uniforms, if a wrestler reports to the meet with an improper uniform, objectionable pads or improper grooming, he may not wrestle until proper corrections have been made. Wrestlers will be charged with a technical violation as well as a time-out to correct the situation. Correction must occur within one and a half minutes for the wrestler to be eligible to wrestle, or a forfeit is declared.

Scorers and Timers

Meeting with the scorers and timers and making certain that they fully understand the rules and duties that pertain to them as outlined in the *NFHS Wrestling Rules Book* can eliminate many problems that could occur during a match. Have this book on hand and use it to go over their responsibilities with them. Remind them that for the most part they should communicate only with you during a match. They can communicate with coaches only when you are directly involved. There should be no communication between the scoring table and spectators.

It's permissible for the scorer to wear red and green armbands to aid in communicating with you during the meet. These armbands are a visual cue for you when a question arises concerning position choice or points. By communicating with eye contact and the bands, you might not need to call a time-out.

Dual Meets

When dual meets are held, the random draw is used to select one of the 14 weight classes to determine the order of weight classes. The weight class selected first will determine the order of weight classes for the dual meet. In multidual events, the sequence determined by the draw will be followed for that day's subsequent meet competition; the subsequent dual meet shall begin one weight class beyond the starting weight class of the previous round. The random draw takes place immediately after the weigh-ins and is conducted by the referee or other authorized person.

Just before the beginning of a dual meet, team captains will then report to you for the flip of the disk. This toss determines which individual gets choice of position at the start of the second period and which individual is to report to the scorer's table first for each weight class.

Here are some final thoughts on carrying out your premeet duties when you are the referee:

- Go about your premeet duties in a businesslike manner. Efficient and effective handling of those duties sends the proper message to coaches and wrestlers. There is no excuse for not getting into the locker rooms to take care of the necessary premeet duties.
- At dual meets, coaches have the responsibility to see that their teams are in the locker room for your premeet visit. Many times you will be able to detect and modify improper padding or bracing without interrupting a match.
- Don't communicate with any spectators. Such communication creates concern about your impartiality and sends the wrong message to wrestlers, coaches and fans.

Assistant Referee Responsibilities

While some state associations don't require that meets have assistant referees, it is encouraged. Having two capable officials on the mat reduces errors in rules interpretation and application. An assistant referee is given the same mobility as a referee and assists the referee in making calls. If you are an assistant referee, your responsibilities are as follows:

- Before the match, assist the referee in checking wrestlers, equipment and uniforms.
- Be aware of the clock and make certain that it starts when the match starts.
- Confirm the match score at the conclusion of each period.
- Be careful not to bring attention to yourself. All attention should be focused on the wrestlers. If you have a concern about a particular call, position yourself close to the referee and state your opinion. Don't signal or make a comment that anyone other than the referee can see or hear. However, there are a few times when a signal from the assistant is appropriate—for example, you should immediately signal interlocking or overlapping of hands or grasping of clothing.

The wrestlers gain immensely when officials use proper positioning to fulfill their duty to ensure a fair and safe match.

- As the referee awards points, continually verify that points awarded are properly scored. This helps eliminate confusion and causes a match to flow more smoothly.

- In case of injury or other unforeseen circumstances, assist the referee in whatever way necessary. This might include communicating with an athletic trainer, helping with equipment and correcting a scoring problem. A good assistant referee is a real asset, as the referee's responsibility during an injury is to be with the injured wrestler.

With you and the referee doing your best, you can observe all action taking place on the mat. There will be fewer undetected infractions and it will be easier to determine the proper outcome of a match. The wrestlers gain immensely when you and the referee use proper positioning and fulfill your duties.

Postmeet Responsibilities

After the meet, verify the score with the scorer, sign the scorebook, note the actual clock time and exit quickly, leaving the competition area with the other referee. Meet management should provide an escort to see you to the locker room. Steer clear of team benches, coaches, wrestlers and fans; don't give anyone a chance to vent their frustrations on you, nor should you begin to socialize with coaches, spectators or wrestlers.

After a meet, discuss critical rulings with the other referee. Let him know what he did well and what he could have done better, and solicit that same information about your performance. Should a coach have questions or comments, respond in a professional manner. Away from the gym, report in writing any disqualifications and unusual incidents to the proper authorities.

Later, evaluate your performance. Did you apply the rules appropriately and consistently? Did you miss some calls? Was your positioning good? Did you maintain control of each match? Did you protect the wrestlers? Were there altercations between opposing wrestlers, and if so how did you handle them? How did you handle rough or violent action? Did you communicate appropriately with coaches, wrestlers and your fellow referee? What did you do well, and how could you improve?

Wrestling is not an easy sport to officiate. Don't be too hard on yourself, but do use your meets as a way to assess your performance and consider how to improve. A great way to improve is to ask a veteran referee to observe you during a meet and then meet with that referee afterward to discuss your performance.

Just as wrestlers aren't perfect, neither are referees. Be as prepared as possible, and use each meet as a learning experience. Consider your performance from a positive standpoint: Think about what you did well and how you can improve.

We've moved from principles of officiating to general meet responsibilities and procedures. The next step is considering calls and responsibilities during matches, which we will cover in the next chapter.

PART II

OFFICIATING WRESTLING MECHANICS

CHAPTER 3

MATCH CALLS AND RESPONSIBILITIES

We've looked at general officiating responsibilities. Now we'll get specific and dive into match responsibilities and calls, including communicating verbally and through signals, getting into and maintaining proper positioning to make calls, and actually making the calls.

This chapter guides you through what you'll encounter in a match. It goes over starting a match, awarding points, calling stalemates, and conducting the end of a period and a match. In other words, this chapter provides the essentials for calling a match expertly.

Communication

Good communication is essential to being a good referee. You might know the sport well, but if you can't communicate what you know, you aren't a good referee. You need to know how to communicate with your fellow referee, scorers and timers, as well as coaches, wrestlers and other officials.

When you are working with another referee, make sure your communication is smooth. Most of your communication will be verbal; however, the assistant referee will use a visual signal when one wrestler locks his hands around his opponent's body and your partner doesn't see it.

If the assistant referee disagrees with the referee, he should communicate this immediately, though the referee shouldn't stop the match unless it's necessary. As referee, you should never interrupt the match when significant action is in progress. If necessary, you may meet at the edge of the mat near the scorer's table to discuss the issue quickly. Do not become involved in a prolonged discussion. In cases of disagreement, the referee has the final decision.

You also need to work closely with the scorers and timers. Should there be any change of scoring or timing, it's your duty to inform the scorer's table and coaches of the change. (The referee, the assistant referee and the two wrestlers are the only people permitted on the mat. Coaches may only address the referee; they are not allowed to communicate with the assistant referee, scorer or timer.)

Signaling is another significant method for communicating calls. You signal and whistle when communicating calls, such as starting a match (see figure 3.1), when stopping a match (see figure 3.2), when starting the injury clock (see figure 3.3) and when stopping the injury clock (see figure 3.4). The sound of the whistle should always be clear and precise. Since the sound of the whistle begins and ends all wrestling, it should be loud enough for all to hear and should not be faltering. The official's hand and arm should move to confirm to the scorer's table that the match has started.

FIGURE 3.1   Referee signaling to start the match.

FIGURE 3.2   Referee signaling to stop the match.

Referees signal numerous other calls as well. All signals are illustrated in the appendix which begins on page 119. Learn these signals well and practice executing them cleanly so that timers, scorers, coaches, wrestlers and fans know what you're communicating. When awarding points, the hand should be held well above the head and very slowly rotated so that the fingers may be seen at all angles.

FIGURE 3.3   Referee signaling to start the injury clock.

FIGURE 3.4   Referee signaling to stop the injury clock.

Positioning

You should always be in position to clearly view any potentially dangerous situations, near falls, falls and illegal holds (see figure 3.5). You also need to be able to see when any points are scored. Finally, your position can help you assess whether a wrestler is stalling.

FIGURE 3.5   Referee in position to view a near fall or fall.

Your understanding and execution of positioning will improve as you gain experience. Positioning is more art than science; it is all about moving around to gain the best view of the action. A referee should always keep an appropriate distance from the action. The distance should be far enough away during times of action to allow for good overall view, yet should not be so close as to interfere with the action. Moves and countermoves also happen quickly and you have to be in position to see them. For example, you have to be able to move quickly and expertly to the proper position to begin the count for a fall as shown in figure 3.5. At times it is almost impossible to see both shoulders because the wrestler's limbs or head are in your way. When you aren't in a good position, in effect you penalize the attacking wrestler because he has to hold the position while waiting for you to begin your count.

Referee Coverage

One of your duties as referee is to start a match. In this section we'll detail how to start a match when wrestlers begin in a neutral or down position and how to resume a match from a starting position. But first, we'll cover how to handle a forfeit, which occurs at the beginning of a match.

A wrestler receives a forfeit when his opponent fails to appear for the match. To receive a forfeit, the wrestler must appear on the mat in uniform, ready to wrestle. At that time you should raise his hand and his team will be credited with the match.

Neutral Position

When you start a match from the neutral position (see figure 3.6), the wrestlers should be between you and the scorer's table. Face the scorer's table as you indicate to the wrestlers to shake hands (a solid handshake, not a hand slap). Look to the scorer's table, sound the whistle as you give a hand signal and then direct your full attention to the match. You must give both visible and audible signals to start the match.

While the wrestlers are maneuvering in a neutral position, you should be in position to look between the two wrestlers as much as possible. As the wrestlers move around you should stay between them and the nearest boundary line. Your positioning may help deter stalling because, debatably, if a referee is positioned close to the out-of-bounds line, the wrestlers may stay in bounds, encouraging wrestling to continue. When the wrestlers are near the mat's edge, be in position to see the supporting parts of both wrestlers as well as the edge of the mat (see figure 3.7). Many times you can prevent an injury when your position keeps a wrestler from contacting the floor, bleachers or scorer's table.

FIGURE 3.6   Referee positioning with wrestlers beginning in the neutral position.

FIGURE 3.7   Referee in position for an out-of-bounds call.

Maintaining Visual Contact

Always strive to keep visual contact with the wrestlers on the mat. When they go out of bounds, continue to maintain eye contact. This will help eliminate pushing, shoving, taunting or any other unsporting behavior. With your presence and eye contact, you can keep these incidents to a minimum. A little prevention on your part will help uphold good sporting behavior throughout the match. When you need to go to the scorer's table, instruct the wrestlers to remain in the 10-foot (3-meter) circle. While at the scorer's table, position yourself so that you can make eye contact with the wrestlers from time to time.

While the wrestlers are on their feet you will move from one side of the mat to the other to maintain a full view of both wrestlers. Stay at a distance where you do not interfere with the wrestlers' moves but are close enough to control difficult situations. Pay particular attention to the following:

- Does either wrestler stall by not making an aggressive move to take the opponent down?
- Does either play the edge of the mat?
- Does either intentionally back off the mat to avoid a takedown?
- Does either push the other off the mat?

Both wrestlers should make every effort to remain inbounds. When you feel that a wrestler has failed to make this effort, penalize him.

When the wrestlers are entwined on the mat, observe from the front, near the heads. Be close enough to have a good view of the hands but not so close as to hinder the wrestlers' movements. Sometimes you'll need to get down on the mat to check for locking hands or questionable maneuvers. Remember to continually move to gain the best vantage point.

Down Position

For the down position the defensive wrestler gets into a legal position and then the offensive wrestler assumes a legal position. When you start the wrestlers from the down position, you may be in front of or behind the wrestlers (see figure 3.8). It is important that you establish eye contact with the scorer's table and give a hand signal immediately after you sound the whistle. You will then direct your full attention to the wrestlers. You must make sure that neither wrestler gains an advantage over his opponent before the whistle sounds. Contestants must be stationary before you start the match.

FIGURE 3.8 Referee positioning with wrestlers beginning in the down position.

Resuming a Match

When the match begins from the down position, station yourself in front of the wrestlers. The positioning for resuming a match is the same as starting the match in the down position, as shown in figure 3.8. Occasionally, too, you might place yourself behind the wrestlers, but it's best to see the face and head because more infractions occur in that area. Always establish eye contact with the scorer's table before starting the match.

Assistant Referee Coverage

Before and following a match, position yourself so that the wrestlers are between you and the referee. A good guideline is to be the first one on the mat and the last one off. When wrestling begins, the assistant

FIGURE 3.9   Assistant referee positions to mirror the referee's positioning.

referee mirrors the location of the referee. When the referee moves, the assistant referee moves, staying 180 degrees from the referee—except when covering the edge of a mat—with a short five-foot (two-meter) boundary (see figure 3.9).

When wrestlers are in the starting positions, you should be opposite or at a slight angle to the referee and look for infractions of the starting position. Call any infraction to the referee's attention. You should always be in a position where you can see the referee, wrestlers, clock and scoreboard.

Remain upright and let the referee make the decision on the near fall or fall. Try to take a position at the feet of the defensive wrestler, observing any possible illegal activity such as finger pulling, grasping of clothing and illegal holds. Communicate the time left in the period to the referee. If the referee has to go to the table, remain in the 10-foot (3-meter) circle with the wrestlers.

At the match's conclusion, stay back but keep the wrestlers between the scoring table and yourself. You should be able to see both coaching areas and the scorer's table.

Awarding Points

As referee, you will award points in a variety of situations for a variety of executions. You need to understand how control and reaction time affect scoring, and you need to know when to award points for takedowns, escapes, reversals, near falls and falls.

For individual matches, points are awarded as follows (for dual meet and tournament scoring, see your *NFHS Wrestling Rules Book*):

- Takedown—2 points
- Escape—1 point
- Reversal—2 points
- Near falls—2 or 3 points

Before we look at the maneuvers, let's consider two important factors in scoring points: control and reaction time.

Control

Control determines the awarding of points. A wrestler who has control of his opponent and can maintain restraining power over him is at an advantage. Control changes when there is a takedown (gaining control), an escape (losing control) or a reversal (changing control).

Often it is difficult to determine when control has been gained, lost or changed. Control is felt as well as observed, so experience as a wrestler will help you understand it. To gain a feel for control, consider attending practice sessions and getting on the mat with coaches and wrestlers.

Certain guidelines should also be helpful:

- In a takedown with a legal headlock and the wrestlers on the mat, control is gained when the defensive wrestler places a foot or hip on the mat in an attempt to stay off the back (see figure 3.10, a and b).
- In a double leg, when the countering wrestler is seated on the mat you should award a takedown as soon as he is no longer able to use his legs for support (see figure 3.10c).
- In a stand up, when the defensive wrestler turns and faces the opponent there is no loss of control, provided the offensive wrestler locks hands and contains his opponent in an upright position (see figure 3.10d).
- However, if the defensive wrestler is able to break this lock by bending at the waist as he faces his opponent, there is a definite loss of control (see figure 3.10e).

FIGURE 3.10   *(a)* Defensive wrestler losing control by placing a foot on the mat, *(b)* defensive wrestler losing control by placing a hip on the mat, *(c)* defensive wrestler losing control when he is no longer able to use his legs for support, *(d)* offensive wrestler locking hands and containing his opponent in an upright position, *(e) defensive* wrestler breaking a lock by bending at the waist.

In a shoulder roll, for example, any time one leg and arm are trapped, you should look for signs of a change in control. A change of control occurs when the defensive wrestler picks up his opponent's lower leg and controls an arm and leg. In the shoulder roll situation, a change of control also occurs when the offensive wrestler becomes more concerned about avoiding being pinned than controlling his opponent.

In the neutral position, wrestlers often use the whizzer maneuver as a countermove and can gain control over their opponent with it. In such situations, change of control is not always easy to determine. A whizzer occurs when a wrestler wraps his arm around the opponent's arm while the opponent is attempting a move such as a single leg or double leg. The wrestler executing the whizzer pulls up as he uses his hips to try to throw his opponent. Again, you will feel as well as observe control.

Reaction Time

Reaction time is generally a silent, two-second count. It usually comes into play when a wrestler, from a neutral position, brings his opponent to the mat with his hands locked around the body or when the defensive wrestler stands and the offensive wrestler locks his hands around the body to bring his opponent to the mat. In these situations, hands locked around the body are legal until the wrestlers come to the down position, at which time the offensive wrestler must release his lock or receive a one-point penalty for a technical violation. The wrestler has a two-second reaction time to release his lock.

Whenever the offensive wrestler locks hands around his opponent's body or both legs while the wrestlers are on the mat, locked hands must be called immediately and no reaction time is permitted. The rules, however, do allow wrestling to continue when a technical violation of locked hands occurs during an escape or reversal. In this situation the referee signals locked hands but provides time for the defensive wrestler to complete his escape or reversal. If the defensive wrestler is successful, award the point(s) earned as well as the penalty for locked hands without stopping the action. If the attempt fails, stop the wrestling and award one point for the technical violation.

A wrestler may legally lock hands once he has met near-fall criteria or if his opponent has all of his weight supported by his feet. Other holds provide no reaction time for locked hands and must immediately be penalized as illegal. For example, a full nelson, chest cradle, strangle hold or locked hands behind the back in a double arm bar from the front are illegal upon application.

Takedown (Two Points)

A takedown occurs when, from the neutral position, a wrestler gains control over his opponent while the supporting parts of either wrestler are inbounds or at least the feet of the scoring wrestler finish down on the mat inbounds (see figure 3.11). As soon as you believe the wrestler has gained control, award points for a takedown by raising your arm with the corresponding wristband of the wrestler scoring the takedown. Raise your arm high above your head with two fingers extended to indicate the number of points. Call out the points and rotate your wrist 90 degrees so your signal can be seen from all directions.

FIGURE 3.11   Wrestler scoring a takedown.

Escape (One Point)

The defensive wrestler earns an escape when he gains a neutral position and his opponent loses control while the supporting parts of either wrestler are inbounds (see figure 3.12, a and b). Award one point in the same manner as a takedown or reversal, extending one finger to indicate one point scored.

a

b

FIGURE 3.12   *(a)* Defensive wrestler in the offensive wrestler's control. *(b)* Defensive wrestler escaping offensive wrestler's control.

Reversal (Two Points)

To earn a reversal, the defensive wrestler must come from underneath and gain control of his opponent either on the mat or in a rear standing position while the supporting parts of either wrestler are inbounds or at least the feet of the scoring contestant finish down on the mat inbounds (see figure 3.13, a and b). Indicate a reversal in the same manner as a takedown.

FIGURE 3.13   (*a and b*) Wrestler earning a reversal.

Near Falls (Two or Three Points) and Falls

Near falls and falls are among the most difficult calls you'll face. Many matches are won or lost when officials improperly award near-fall points. This typically occurs because the referee failed to get in position quickly enough to observe the entire situation.

Often the contestants are so entangled that it is difficult to see whether a wrestler is pinned. When calling a fall, don't begin the count until you can see the shoulders or scapulas touching the mat or you see the defensive wrestler held in a high bridge (see figure 3.14, a and b).

a

b

FIGURE 3.14 (*a*) Referee beginning the count when he sees the shoulders or scapulas touching the mat or (*b*) the defensive wrestler in a high bridge.

Most falls and near falls occur within a few seconds, so you have to be ready to immediately change your position to get the best vantage point. Don't award a wrestler points for a near fall until the situation has ended. A fall can occur at any time and with unorthodox holds. Regardless of the position, either wrestler can be awarded a fall if the requirements are met.

Awarding a Near Fall Make sure you don't award a near fall until the defensive wrestler has escaped a pinning situation or the period ends. You can award points only once for a pinning situation, but the offensive wrestler can create more than one pinning situation, entitling him to additional points. It's up to you to determine when one pinning situation ends and another begins. When the defensive wrestler is free and the offensive wrestler changes his attack, the situation has ended. Don't rely completely on the action of the bottom wrestler; also observe what the offensive wrestler is doing to change moves.

Be alert, be in position and anticipate situations before they arise. Sometimes during a flurry of action an inexperienced official gives points too quickly. As soon as a near-fall situation has concluded, raise your arm with the wristband corresponding to the scoring contestant, extend the proper number of fingers (two or three) and tap your shoulder (see figure 3.15, a and b). This tapping indicates that near-fall points were earned. For example, one wrestler has his opponent in a pinning combination

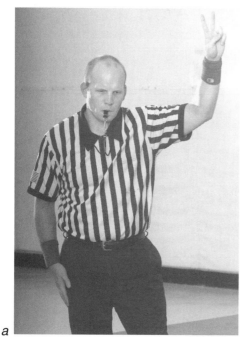

a   b

FIGURE 3.15   (*a and b*) Official indicating a near fall.

that has one shoulder in contact with the mat and the other within four inches. A two-point near fall would be called if the referee counts to four seconds when the opponent manages to turn his stomach and a three-point near fall would be called if, in the same situation, the referee had counted to five seconds.

Determining a Fall   To determine a fall, get down on the mat so you can see both shoulders or scapulas touching the mat. After you make the two-second silent count, sound your whistle and strike the mat hard with the palm of your hand (see figure 3.16). Don't raise your hand until the fall is complete because doing so indicates that a fall has occurred and the match is over. Be aware of the time left in the period and listen for the buzzer to determine whether the fall occurred before or after it.

FIGURE 3.16   Official indicating a fall.

Out of Bounds

Make out-of-bounds decisions based on the wrestlers' positions and the type of action going on. Work hard to maintain the best position as wrestlers approach the mat's edge. Try to get in a position on the out-of-bounds side where you can see between the wrestlers. Do all you can to be in position to stop any potentially dangerous or illegal holds. Use proper signals so that fans, wrestlers and coaches will understand what is happening on the mat.

Know where the boundary line is and exactly where the wrestlers are on the mat. Wrestlers are inbounds if the supporting parts of either wrestler are inside the boundary lines. When a takedown is in progress and the wrestlers are in a neutral position, again, wrestling should continue as long as the supporting parts of either wrestler remain within the boundary lines.

When awarding a takedown at the edge of the mat, award points when a wrestler establishes control while the supporting parts of either wrestler are inbounds or at least the feet of the scoring contestant finish down on the mat inbounds (see figure 3.17). Whenever possible, award points on edge-of-mat calls before blowing the whistle for out of bounds.

If the defensive wrestler initiates a move near a boundary but is unable to complete it because both contestants go out of bounds, one of the wrestlers may have earned escape points. Award an escape when the offensive wrestler loses control while his opponent is still inbounds or when the defensive wrestler is unable to gain control before going out of bounds. This is not a reversal because both wrestlers went out of bounds before the defensive wrestler could gain control.

If neither wrestler has control while the supporting parts of one remain inbounds, the wrestlers are in a neutral position. In a reversal at the edge of the mat, a wrestler must establish control while the supporting parts of either wrestler are inbounds or at least the feet of the scoring contestant finish down on the mat inbounds.

FIGURE 3.17   Wrestler establishing control with supporting parts still inbounds.

Injuries and Defaults

Wrestlers are injured through illegal holds or action and legal holds or action. In a moment we'll address how to respond in each situation, but first let's cover some concerns that are related to injury situations:

- Coaches have the ethical responsibility not to permit wrestlers to win matches by claiming injury unless they are injured to the extent that they should not continue. Taking an injury time-out for a noninjury is unethical.

- During time-outs, no more than two attendants and a physician are permitted on the mat to attend a wrestler. During this time wrestlers can be given refreshment.

- Any contestant who is bleeding will be charged with bleeding time. The number of time-outs for bleeding is left to your discretion. If bleeding is not controlled within a cumulative time of five minutes, the match is over. In any bleeding situation, bleeding should be controlled first; then injury or recovery time can be used.

Injured by Illegal Hold

When a wrestler is injured by an illegal hold, stop the match and verbally and physically signal (see figure 3.18) that the hold was illegal. Allow a two-minute recovery time for the injured wrestler. Recovery time is the

FIGURE 3.18   Referee signaling an illegal hold.

time allowed "to recover" from an injury that is the result of an illegal hold, unnecessary roughness or unsportsmanlike conduct. The time required to treat an injury from illegal action is not deducted from the wrestler's injury time. A wrestler cannot take injury time immediately following recovery time. If a contestant is unable to wrestle following his recovery time, award the injured wrestler the match by default.

When a wrestler is injured by an illegal hold and decides to continue after a short recovery time, he cannot later claim to be unable to continue because of the injury and thereby win the match by default.

Injured by Legal Hold

When a wrestler is injured by a legal hold, he is entitled to an injury time-out of one and a half minutes. If he is unable to continue after the time-out, award his opponent the match by default. Injury time cannot immediately precede or follow recovery time.

A wrestler who has been apparently rendered unconscious cannot resume wrestling after regaining consciousness without the written approval of a physician (MD or DO). If no physician is present, do not permit the contestant to wrestle. If the attending physician recommends that a wrestler not continue even though consciousness was not involved, then no one, including you, the coach or a parent, can overrule the physician.

When the injury time-out ends, wrestlers return to their appropriate starting positions as if they had gone out of bounds.

Additional Concerns

In addition to communication, position, points, out-of-bounds situations, and injuries and defaults, there are some other situations you need to be aware of, including

- stalemates,
- displaced ear guards, and
- the end of the period and the match.

Stalemates

Sometimes wrestlers get locked up and the action grinds to a near halt because neither wrestler is able to make a move. The action often slows as wrestlers come together, but at times it slows to a point where a stalemate occurs. A stalemate takes place in the following situations:

- Contestants are interlocked in a position in which neither wrestler can improve his position.

- Either competitor has his hands locked around one leg of the opponent to prevent scoring.
- The offensive wrestler applies a grapevine and is unable to turn the opponent.

In each of these situations, you should stop the match, signal a stalemate and then have the wrestlers resume as if they had gone out of bounds. If a wrestler uses either of the last two maneuvers two or three times, you should warn him for stalling.

Here are a few examples of stalemates:

- The top wrestler has a waist and ankle ride and the bottom wrestler attempts an inside switch. The top wrestler flattens out so that the bottom wrestler cannot complete the switch and the top wrestler cannot move without giving up his advantage (see figure 3.19).
- Both wrestlers are in a neutral position, flattened out following an attempted single leg. Neither will move because to do so would result in a takedown.

FIGURE 3.19
Wrestler in a stalemate.

- The defensive wrestler uses a whizzer and the offensive wrestler counters by grasping the opponent's ankle (see figure 3.20).

There are many other situations in which a stalemate could occur. You should focus on recognizing a stalemate, stopping the match and resuming it as if the wrestlers had gone out of bounds.

Displaced Ear Guards

Protective ear guards are part of a wrestler's uniform. While the ear guards must be securely fastened, they can occasionally be displaced during competition.

Use good judgment in stopping a match to replace ear guards. Never put a wrestler at a disadvantage or force a wrestler to forfeit an advantage because his ear guards slipped. If the ear guard is completely off, stop the match when no significant action is in progress and allow the wrestler to replace the equipment.

End of Periods and Matches

At the end of the first period, ask the wrestler with the choice of position to select a position—neutral, top, bottom—or defer. This clarifies the

FIGURE 3.20   Stalemate from a whizzer.

wrestler's choices. Following the end of the second period, the wrestler who did not have the choice will choose neutral, top or bottom to begin the third period. The wrestler should make his choice immediately, and once you accept the decision, it cannot be changed.

A match lasts from the start of the first period until the conclusion of wrestling. The end-of-match procedure is simply a means of letting everyone know the results. When the match ends by a fall, call the contestants to the center of the mat, have them shake hands and raise the arm of the winner. When the match does not end by a fall, direct the contestants to remain in the circle and then check with the scorer's table. Once the points have been reviewed, return to the center of the mat, direct the contestants to shake hands and raise the hand of the winner (see figure 3.21). The handshake should be firm and traditional.

FIGURE 3.21   Referee declaring the winner.

In this chapter we focused on match responsibilities and calls. In the next chapter we'll consider another aspect of officiating matches: enforcing the rules when you encounter infractions.

CHAPTER 4

ENFORCING INFRACTIONS

In the last chapter we looked at the calls you make during matches. In this chapter we continue to discuss calls, focusing on infractions. We'll cover illegal holds, potentially dangerous holds, violations, stalling, cautions, coaches' conduct and sportsmanship.

Illegal Holds and Potentially Dangerous Holds

The wrestlers' safety is one of your primary concerns. Any hold that endangers life or limb is illegal; any act that goes beyond aggressive wrestling becomes unnecessary roughness. Some holds are legitimate but potentially dangerous. It is of the utmost importance that you thoroughly understand illegal acts and potentially dangerous holds.

Your decision to stop a match hinges on two factors: whether a hold is illegal and whether it is dangerous. If it is illegal, stop the match and penalize the offending wrestler. If it is dangerous, warn the offending wrestler, and if he does not heed the warning, stop the match and penalize him. Be careful in your decision to stop a match; when you do so for any reason other than those just specified, you might eliminate a wrestler's advantage, particularly in a pinning situation. This could give the defensive wrestler an unfair chance for a new start.

There are also times when the opponent's action can turn a wrestler's legal hold into an illegal hold. When this occurs, you might have to stop the action without penalizing either wrestler. When trying to turn his opponent while applying a cross-body ride, a wrestler has to loosen his legs so that the opponent can turn to avoid injury. Any time the defensive wrestler is unable to turn to avoid injury, you should break the action with no penalty and restart the wrestlers.

Illegal Holds

Illegal holds have no place in wrestling. You need to do all you can to prevent them and move in quickly to stop them when they occur. These holds are dangerous and are a black eye on the sport. Illegal holds include the following as shown in figure 4.1, a through p.

FIGURE 4.1   *(a)* Salto, suplay or any variation that meets slam criteria.

FIGURE 4.1   *(b)* Double underhook snapback from the standing position.

FIGURE 4.1   *(c)* Hammerlock above a right angle.

FIGURE 4.1   *(d)* Twisting hammerlock.

FIGURE 4.1   *(e)* Straight head scissor even though an arm is included.

FIGURE 4.1
(f) Full nelson.

FIGURE 4.1
(g) Strangle
hold.

FIGURE 4.1
(h) Twisting
knee lock.

FIGURE 4.1
(i) Overhead
double arm bar
with one or both
arms.

FIGURE 4.1 *(j)* Locking the hands behind the back in a double arm bar from the front.

FIGURE 4.1 *(k)* Neck wrench.

FIGURE 4.1 *(l)* Front quarter nelson with the chin.

FIGURE 4.1 *(m)* Leg block (cut back).

FIGURE 4.1   *(n)* Backbow.

FIGURE 4.1   *(o)* Overscissor when pressure is applied against the joint.

FIGURE 4.1   *(p)* Figure 4 around the body or both legs.

Other illegal holds can include but are not limited to the following:

- Body slam
- Intentional drill or forceful fallback
- Pulling back the thumb or one, two or three fingers
- Headlock in which the arms or hands are locked around the opponent's head without encircling a leg or an arm at or above the elbow (except in the guillotine after near-fall criteria have been met or in the three-quarter nelson
- Keylock

- Bending, twisting or forcing the head or any limb beyond its normal limit of movement
- Punishing hold
- Hold where there is pressure over the mouth, nose, throat or neck that restricts breathing or circulation

Potentially Dangerous Holds

Potentially dangerous holds force a body part to the limit of its normal range of movement. Caution wrestlers who apply such a hold before the hold becomes illegal. You should immediately stop a match in these situations:

- When a hold becomes illegal; penalize the wrestler accordingly.
- When a legal hold becomes dangerous. Assign no penalty and resume the match as following an out-of-bounds situation. Follow this procedure when a wrestler uses a potentially dangerous hold with such force that it endangers the opponent or when it becomes an unintentionally punishing hold.
- When a wrestler continues a potentially dangerous hold after you have verbally cautioned him.

Following are examples of two positions you need to be aware of: headlocks and control of arms. Both situations are potentially dangerous, so you need to know what to look for and when to stop the hold.

Headlocks   All headlocks are potentially dangerous. Whenever a head-lock is applied, as shown in figure 4.2, you need to be especially alert to the pressure exerted on the throat or neck and anticipate the action; it can move quickly. Because of the dangers it presents, make sure you are in position to observe the hold carefully. With the application of a front headlock you may have to adjust your position by changing levels for a better look at the pressure applied.

A headlock with an arm encircled above the elbow or leg encircled is legal but potentially dangerous. Sometimes the arm encircling the head restricts the defensive wrestler's breathing or circulation. The defensive wrestler's face might be forced tightly into his chest or into the side of the offensive wrestler, restricting the defensive wrestler's breathing. Or the defensive wrestler's head and shoulder might be forced together to the extent that the shoulder puts pressure on the jugular vein or carotid artery, a very dangerous situation that might not be obvious to you. Finally, the strength of the wrestler applying the headlock might twist, constrict or compact the neck, resulting in potentially serious damage.

FIGURE 4.2 Wrestler executing a legal headlock.

When a headlock is applied it is very important that you keep the safety of the wrestlers in mind. Should you be in doubt as to the legality of the headlock, stop the action and start again, even if the defensive wrestler is on his back close to a pin.

The nature of the headlock prevents the defensive wrestler from indicating pain or distress when his opponent is of equal or superior strength. You must be very alert during such situations because there might be no visible sign of distress until the defensive wrestler loses consciousness. Be ready to prevent a potentially dangerous headlock from becoming illegal or causing injury.

Control of Arms Another potentially dangerous situation exists when the defensive wrestler is standing and the offensive wrestler has control of one or both of his opponent's arms. Examples of upper-body arm locks include arm bars when the offensive wrestler steps in front for a forward trip, double arm bars, half nelsons and arm bars, and chicken wings (see figure 4.3, a through d). When the offensive wrestler attempts to bring the defensive wrestler back to the mat, caution the offensive wrestler that there is no way the defensive wrestler can protect himself when his arms are tied up. If you feel there is potential for injury, stop the match to protect the defensive wrestler.

FIGURE 4.3   *(a)* Arm bar when the offensive wrestler steps in front for a forward trip, *(b)* double arm bar, *(c)* half nelson and arm bar, *(d)* chicken wing.

Violations

Violations occur in a variety of situations. Some violations have to do with stalling, others have to do with illegal moves or starting positions, and others are related to pinning situations or when a wrestler is attempting an escape or reversal. It is your duty to recognize all potential violations when they occur and assign penalties, such as a warning or caution, appropriately. Be firm in enforcing both the letter and the spirit of the rules, and penalize violations promptly and consistently. Stop the match and penalize violations, except in these situations:

- *Stalling*. At the first occurrence of stalling, warn a wrestler without issuing a penalty. Also issue a warning whenever stalling occurs in the neutral position, giving a verbal warning and the proper signal. Don't stop a match for a warning or penalty while the wrestlers are in the neutral position, and don't stop the match to warn the offensive wrestler when the defensive wrestler has come to the standing position (see the following section on stalling for more information).

- *False starts or illegal starting positions.* The first two times a wrestler has a false start or is in an illegal starting position, caution the wrestler without issuing a penalty.
- *Pinning.* In a pinning situation, don't stop the match to penalize the defensive wrestler; stop the match after the situation has concluded. However, if a wrestler might get injured, stop the match and award the appropriate points. Signal the points to be awarded and the wrestler to whom they are awarded, and announce the penalty so that wrestlers, scorers, coaches and spectators are aware of the infraction.
- *Escapes or reversals.* Use the interlocking hand signal when the offensive wrestler locks his hands around or grasps the clothing of the defensive wrestler who is attempting an escape or reversal. Stop the match only when it is apparent that the defensive wrestler will not complete the escape or reversal. If the defensive wrestler is successful, don't stop the match to award points.
- *Takedowns.* Issue a warning when a wrestler uses a figure 4 scissors around the opponent's head from the neutral position and a takedown is imminent. Stop the match only when it is obvious that the takedown will not be completed. If the takedown is successful, don't stop the match to award points. When a wrestler grasps the clothing of the opponent being taken down and a takedown is imminent, stop the match only when it is obvious that the takedown will not be completed. If the takedown is successful, don't stop the match to award points.

For all other violations, stop the match and announce the penalty using the NFHS Officiating Wrestling signals, as shown in the appendix beginning on page 119, in addition to verbalizing the call, so that coaches, wrestlers, scorers and spectators are all aware of the penalty.

Stalling

Wrestlers must make an honest effort to stay within the 10-foot (3-meter) circle and wrestle aggressively regardless of position, time or score. Wrestlers are equally responsible for initiating action, no matter their position. In this section we'll explore the necessity of removing stalling from the sport, factors that lead to stalling and how to handle stalling.

Coaches and officials must make every effort to discourage factors that contibute to stalling. In the neutral position, it is the responsibility of both contestants to make every effort to stay within the 10-foot circle, make contact, set up a takedown and attempt a takedown. A wrestler can circle to set up the takedown, but backing away from the opponent, avoiding contact and playing the edge of the mat are all examples of stalling.

When the wrestlers are in the neutral position near a boundary and it becomes apparent that a competitor is stepping out of bounds to avoid a move by the opponent, warn the wrestler immediately. If you have already issued the wrestler a warning, penalize him for stalling. (Penalize a wrestler one point for each of his first two penalties, two points for his third penalty and disqualify him for his fourth penalty.)

Holds or actions that tend to contribute to stalling in the neutral position are as follows:

- Performing upper-body tie-ups with no attempt to take down the opponent
- Blocking with the forearm or head against the chest or clavicle
- Faking contact
- Grasping one leg and holding it without following through for an attempted takedown
- Controlling the opponent's hand and wrist and not following through with an attempted takedown

Removing Stalling

Stalling must be removed from wrestling. Coaches, wrestlers and officials share this responsibility. Coaches are responsible for teaching aggressive wrestling, requiring their wrestlers to work for the fall at all times. Wrestlers are charged with wrestling aggressively, whether in the top, bottom or neutral position. Officials must be firm in enforcing the stalling rule; they must consistently and without hesitation penalize any stalling infraction. All three groups must work together to ensure that wrestling remains an exciting sport.

Recognizing Stalling

When you recognize stalling, warn the offender. Without hesitation, penalize the offending wrestler if he stalls again. Officials have the responsibility to eliminate stalling by enforcing the letter of the rule.

The rest of this section describes many situations in which a wrestler might be stalling. Watch for these situations and be ready to penalize stalling when you see it.

Releasing an Opponent Intentionally releasing an opponent is not considered stalling unless the wrestler with the advantage is not wrestling aggressively. The intentional release and takedown method of building up points is within the rules as long as the offensive wrestler releases the opponent, moves to the front and faces the opponent before attempting a takedown.

Working for a Fall   The offensive wrestler must make an honest effort to work for a fall. Whenever the offensive wrestler holds the opponent on the mat without moving up to a perpendicular position and working for a fall, he is stalling. It is not sufficient to merely move to a perpendicular position, because the wrestler can hold the opponent on the mat without working for the fall. Any time the wrestler in the advantage position is content to hold the opponent down or keep the opponent off base without working for a fall, he is stalling.

Holds and positions that tend to contribute to stalling in the advantage position are as follows:

- Being content to ride the opponent
- Using a double-leg grapevine for riding purposes only (see figure 4.4a)
- Trapping an ankle with the lower leg while using a deep waist (see figure 4.4b)
- Using a deep waist with no attempt to improve position
- Holding an opponent in a cradle without attempting to turn the opponent on his back (see figure 4.4c)
- Shooting a deep half or arm bar and staying parallel after breaking down the opponent
- Repeatedly putting on a grapevine when the opponent stands (see figure 4.4d)
- Staying behind the opponent while standing, making no attempt to bring the opponent to the mat

Attempting an Escape or Reversal   If the wrestler in the defensive position does not try to escape or reverse and he is not being overpowered, he is stalling. The defensive wrestler must be aggressive; he must always work to improve his position. This doesn't mean the defensive wrestler must unnecessarily expose himself to greater disadvantage, but he must make a concerted effort to gain an escape or reversal.

Situations that tend to contribute to stalling in the defensive position are as follows:

- Remaining on all fours in a basic start
- Being content to lie belly down on the mat
- Lying on the mat with elbows held in close to the body
- Grasping the opponent's hands and holding them close to the defendant's body

FIGURE 4.4   *(a)* Double-leg grapevine; *(b)* trapping an ankle with the lower leg; *(c)* cradle; *(d)* repeated grapevine.

During a Tiebreaker   A tiebreaker occurs after the wrestlers have completed a regular match and a one-minute overtime. It presents a unique situation: The next wrestler to score wins. The defensive wrestler could score through escape, reversal or penalty points. Likewise, if the offensive wrestler scores, the match is over. If a wrestler controls his opponent for 30 seconds, the match is finished and the offensive wrestler wins. If a wrestler is penalized for stalling during a tiebreaker, his opponent wins the match.

Issuing Cautions

Assuming an incorrect starting position or making a false start is a technical violation. You should caution a wrestler for his first and second offenses. After the second caution, penalize the wrestler one point for any subsequent technical violations in accordance with the penalty chart in the *NFHS Wrestling Rules Book.*

During tournaments, particularly when simultaneous matches are going on, use common sense regarding cautions and penalties in the starting position. For example, a wrestler who moves at the sound of the whistle coming from an adjoining mat should not be cautioned or penalized for a false start. Consider the extenuating circumstances and enforce the spirit rather than the letter of the rule.

Working With Coaches

Coaches set the tone for how their wrestlers approach matches, conduct themselves on the mat, and behave before and after matches. Coaches are responsible for instructing their athletes and modeling appropriate behavior, which includes how they relate to officials and to all others connected to the sport.

This section reflects on two important officiating issues related to coaching:

- Approaching the scorer's table
- Giving directions to wrestlers

Approaching the Scorer's Table

While a match is in progress, a coach may approach the scorer's table to request a conference to question the misapplication of a rule. You can stop the match when nothing significant is taking place and the coach can voice his concern with you at the scorer's table. A coach may not challenge the official's judgment. Sometimes there is a fine line between questioning the application of a rule or questioning a referee's judgment. A coach may not question a referee's judgment on a stalling call, for example, since stalling is judgment. However, he may ask what criteria you use for stalling. Should you have a doubt regarding the coach's motive, it is best to begin the conference with the question, "What rule do you feel has been misapplied?" This way, you can focus on the rule and not the judgment. In any case, the discussion should take place directly in front of the scorer's table. Additionally, any time that a coach expresses himself in an unsporting manner, he shall be penalized immediately.

When a coach requests that you stop the match, do so at the first opportune moment, when no significant action is occurring. Hear the coach out and then make a decision. If there is no error in the application of the rule or the coach disagrees with your judgment, penalize the coach for misconduct.

Giving Directions to Wrestlers

Wrestling provides coaches close access to their wrestlers on the mat. Coaches and any other team personnel on the bench are allowed to direct and encourage wrestlers on the mat provided they do so in a sporting manner. The next section gives examples of unsporting behavior. The point is, it's okay for coaches to communicate with their wrestlers on the mat as long as the communication follows protocol and doesn't slip into unsporting behavior.

Sporting Behavior

Good sporting behavior in high school wrestling should be a high priority for everyone involved. Everyone needs to concentrate on the ideals of good sporting behavior and genuine concern for others involved in the sport. Such behavior begins with coaches. Head coaches are responsible for the conduct of their wrestlers and all team personnel. If coaches conduct themselves in a sporting manner, their behavior will significantly influence those under their charge. Because of this influence, NFHS has stringent rules about the action of coaches and team personnel in the bench area.

Examples of unsporting acts include

- using an artificial aid such as a megaphone or electronic device to give directions to wrestlers;
- attempting to influence an official's decision;
- disrespectfully addressing an official or objecting to an official's decision;
- baiting, berating or criticizing the opponent; and
- behaving in ways that incite the crowd.

There will be times when wrestlers, coaches and other team personnel won't conduct themselves appropriately. We'll look at how to address unsporting conduct by wrestlers and coaches, flagrant misconduct by wrestlers and coaches, and unsporting fan behavior.

Unsporting Conduct by Wrestlers

Unsporting conduct by wrestlers can be physical or nonphysical and can occur before, during or after a match. Such acts include but are not limited to pushing, shoving, swearing, intimidation, baiting an opponent, throwing ear guards, spitting, indicating displeasure with a call, failing to keep shoulder straps up while on the mat and failing to comply with end-of-match procedures.

In recent years taunting has become a serious problem in high school sports. The NFHS disapproves of any form of taunting, especially when it is intended to embarrass, ridicule or demean others under any circumstances, including on the basis of race, religion, gender or national origin. This type of behavior does not belong in high school wrestling, and you need to be alert for it and take appropriate action, strictly enforcing sporting rules.

In the case of wrestlers, this means deducting a point from the team total for their first offense and deducting two points and ejecting the wrestler for the second offense. Upon ejection, the wrestler should be removed from the premises only if authorized school personnel are available. When the team has only one coach and no school personnel are available to supervise the ejected person, that person must remain on the team bench under the supervision of the head coach.

Unsporting Conduct by Coaches

Unsporting conduct by coaches and other team personnel includes any act that becomes abusive or interferes with the match. This includes poor bench decorum, acts of disrespect or any action that incites a negative reaction in others.

Again, such behavior means you deduct a point from the team total for the first offense and deduct two points and eject the offending party for the second offense.

Flagrant Misconduct

Flagrant misconduct is any act that happens before, during or after a match that you consider to be serious enough to disqualify an individual or coach from the match, dual meet or tournament. For wrestlers, this includes but is not limited to biting, striking, butting, elbowing and kicking an opponent. In addition, continual unsportsmanlike behavior can be viewed as flagrant misconduct. Finally, flagrant misconduct also includes the use of tobacco products.

In all cases of flagrant misconduct, have the offender removed from the premises. Their disqualification and removal should happen on the first offense, and this disqualification costs their team three points. In the case of a multiple-school event or tournament, a disqualified wrestler cannot wrestle for the remainder of the event and no team points can be earned in his spot. Coaches and other team staff cannot return for the remainder of the event, whether it's a dual meet or a tournament.

Unsporting Conduct by Fans

It's best not to respond to fan behavior because it focuses attention on the spectators rather than the wrestlers. However, a spectator who acts in an unsporting manner may be removed from the premises for the remainder of the event. When you request that home management remove a spectator, they are responsible for following through with your request. In such situations, neither team is penalized. Wrestling should resume only after the offender has been removed.

So far we've covered the general principles of officiating and your specific responsibilities and calls. Now we're going to shift gears and put you in the position of applying the rules. In the next four chapters, you will encounter situations in which you must decide how you would rule.

PART III

APPLYING THE RULES

CHAPTER 5

WEIGHT CERTIFICATION, WEIGH-INS AND EQUIPMENT

As you know from the *NFHS Wrestling Rules Book*, there are 10 categories of wrestling rules. In the next four chapters we'll present a number of cases in each category and the appropriate rulings. These cases are meant to supplement close study of the rules and bring to life some of the situations you will face, but they by no means replace the need to thoroughly know the rules book. Make sure you are well versed in all the rules as spelled out in the rules book, and then use these chapters to test and augment your understanding.

In this chapter, we'll consider cases under the first four categories:

- Rule 1: Competition
- Rule 2: Equipment
- Rule 3: Officials and Duties
- Rule 4: Wrestlers' Classification and Weigh-In

Rule 1: Competition

Rule 1 covers rules related to competition. Consider how you would respond in each situation and check your judgments against the answers beginning on page 68.

CASE 1: Wrestling After Winning a Forfeit

During a dual meet with Jamestown, Pittsfield has no one to wrestle at 119 pounds (54 kilograms). The Jamestown coach sends his 119-pound wrestler to the scorer's table and then to the mat to receive forfeit points, which you award by signaling a forfeit. Immediately after your signal, the Jamestown coach approaches the scorer's table and asks that the forfeit be deleted so that his 119-pound, wrestler can wrestle in the 125-pound (57-kilogram) class. What do you rule?

CASE 2: Wrestling in a Different Weight Class
York is wrestling at Brownsburg. York has weighed in two wrestlers for the 215-pound (98-kilogram) class and one wrestler for the 275-pound (125-kilogram) class. After the 215-pound match is over, the York coach sends the other 215-pound wrestler to wrestle the 275-pound match. The Brownsburg coach objects, saying that a different wrestler weighed in for the 275-pound match. How do you rule?

CASE 3: Certified Wrestling Weight
A Centralia wrestler is certified at 130 pounds (59 kilograms) and weighs in for a dual meet against Westwood at 133 pounds (60 kilograms). He wrestles at 140 pounds (64 kilograms) in this meet. By wrestling at this weight, does he lose his certification at 130 pounds?

Rule 2: Equipment

Rule 2 covers situations that involve equipment. Following are a few examples of those situations. As you read them, consider how you would rule and then refer to the answers beginning on page 69 at the end of the chapter.

CASE 4: Team Bench Configuration
As you inspect the mat area before a dual meet, you notice that the team benches are not adjacent to the scorer's table. They are on opposite sides of the mat and each bench is 10 feet (3 meters) from the edge of the mat. Is this permissible, or do the benches need to be moved?

CASE 5: Overloading the Restricted Area
During a tournament, Jamestown's coach and manager occupy the chairs reserved for their use in the restricted area as they prepare to watch their 125-pound (57-kilogram) wrestler in his match. Before the third period begins, you notice that the Jamestown assistant coach has moved into the restricted area, joining the head coach and manager. You inform the Jamestown head coach that only two people can be in the restricted area, and then you move to the center of the mat to restart the match. However, none of the three Jamestown personnel leaves the restricted area. What do you do?

CASE 6: Weighing In on a Digital Scale
Westwood arrives at Pittsfield for a dual meet and discovers that Pittsfield is using a digital scale instead of a balance scale. The Westwood coach protests, saying that a balance scale is necessary for the weigh-ins. How do you respond?

Rule 3: Officials and Duties

Rule 3 covers the duties of the referee, assistant referee, scorer and time-keeper and how to rule in certain situations. We've provided a couple of those situations here; determine how you would rule and then check your answers beginning on page 69 at the end of the chapter.

CASE 7: Flagrant Misconduct Call

Following the 275-pound (125-kilogram) match in which the Centralia wrestler lost a close battle to his York counterpart, you sign the scorebook. Afterward the Centralia wrestler sees you in the hallway on his way to the locker room and uses profanity directed toward you. You issue a flagrant misconduct call against him. Is this the proper call to make?

CASE 8: Equipment Problem in the Case of a Forfeit

Richmond arrives at Brownsburg for a dual meet and presents no wrestler for the 119-pound (54-kilogram) class. Brownsburg weighs in a wrestler at 119 pounds who has a cast on his wrist which does not allow normal range of motion. You were not in charge of the weigh-in and you did not inspect the cast before the 119-pound match.

Following the 112-pound (51-kilogram) match, the Brownsburg wrestler comes onto the mat to receive a forfeit. You notice that his forearm cast is exposed and not properly covered or padded. Do you award him a forfeit?

Rule 4: Wrestlers' Classification and Weigh-In

Rule 4 clarifies wrestlers' classifications and weigh-in procedures. Among the subjects at hand are wrestlers' uniforms, appearance and health, and use of special equipment, as well as weight classes and weigh-ins. Test your knowledge of this rule by considering your responses to the following situations. You'll find the correct answers beginning on page 69 at the end of the chapter.

CASE 9: Wrestling With a Communicable Disease

During the premeet conference at a dual between Westwood and Independence, the Westwood coach presents a letter from a doctor stating that Westwood's 145-pound (66-kilogram) wrestler has a communicable skin condition. The letter goes on to say that there will be no problem as long as the skin is properly covered, and the Westwood coach assures you that this can easily be done. Does the doctor's statement make it okay for the wrestler to compete?

CASE 10: Wrestling With a Knee Brace

A 160-pound (73-kilogram) Richmond wrestler reports to the mat ready to wrestle against his Pittsfield opponent. The Richmond wrestler is wearing a knee brace that is excessively padded and wrapped. Is this legal?

CASE 11: Trying to Make Weight

You arrive at the site of a conference tournament and notice a wrestler running around the gymnasium in a plastic suit, obviously attempting to lose weight before the weigh-in. What do you do?

CASE 12: Late for Weigh-In

Jamestown is hosting Centralia at a dual meet. Weigh-ins begin at 6 p.m. The Jamestown 119-pound (54-kilogram) wrestler fails to show up when his weight is called, so no one for Jamestown weighs in at 119. Just before the final weigh-in, Jamestown's 119-pound wrestler shows up. Should you allow him to weigh in?

Answers

Here are the correct answers in each situation. Compare them with your responses to see how you did.

Case 1: Wrestling After Winning a Forfeit

The Jamestown coach wants the best of both worlds: He wants the forfeit points for his 119-pound wrestler and he wants his 119-pound wrestler to wrestle at 125 pounds. He can't have his cake and eat it, too. Wrestlers can't accept a forfeit in one weight class and then wrestle at another class. The 119-pounder receives the forfeit points but cannot wrestle at 125 pounds.

Case 2: Wrestling in a Different Weight Class

The Brownsburg coach's objections are groundless. The York wrestler who qualified for the 215-pound class and did not wrestle at that class can move up to the 275-pound class, even though another York wrestler qualified at that weight.

Case 3: Certified Wrestling Weight

The Centralia wrestler who is certified at 130 pounds and wrestles in a dual meet at 140 pounds does not lose his certification. He can either wrestle at his certified weight or one weight class up. The Centralia wrestler weighed in at 133 pounds for the meet against Westwood. This makes him a 135-pound (61-kilogram) contestant who can wrestle at either 135 or 140 without losing his 130-pound certification. Had the Centralia wrestler weighed in at 138 pounds (63 kilograms), he would have lost his 130-pound certification because he would have weighed in two classes above 130.

Case 4: Team Bench Configuration

This bench configuration is permissible. At dual meets, team benches are to be at least 10 feet (3 meters) from the mat and at least 10 feet from the scorer's table. It's okay to have team benches on opposite sides of the mat.

Case 5: Overloading the Restricted Area

You told the Jamestown coach that one of the three team personnel had to leave the restricted area, yet no one left. By refusing to comply with your instruction, the Jamestown team is guilty of unsportsmanlike conduct. You should make that call and deduct one team point from Jamestown's score.

Case 6: Weighing In on a Digital Scale

The Westwood coach has no grounds for protest. While he might prefer balance scales and believe them to be more accurate than digital scales, balance scales are not mandatory. The home team simply has to provide scales whose accuracy has been annually certified.

Case 7: Flagrant Misconduct Call

You cannot issue a flagrant misconduct call—or any other call—against the wrestler, even though he cursed at you. Your jurisdiction at dual meets begins when you arrive at the site and ends once you approve the scorebook. Although you can't issue a misconduct call, you should report the incident to the Centralia head coach and the state association office.

Case 8: Equipment Problem in the Case of a Forfeit

If the wrestler can correct the equipment problem within the allotted injury time of one and a half minutes, you should award him the forfeit. If he can't become legal, then you should not grant a forfeit.

It is your responsibility to inspect all supplementary devices, pads and other types of equipment and make the appropriate ruling.

Case 9: Wrestling With a Communicable Disease

No, you should not allow the Westwood wrestler to compete. It doesn't matter what the doctor's letter says; you cannot allow a wrestler with a communicable skin condition to wrestle.

Case 10: Wrestling With a Knee Brace

The legality of the knee brace is your judgment call. It is legal to wear a knee brace as long as any hard or abrasive equipment is padded and covered. However, the equipment must allow for normal joint movement and it cannot prevent the opponent from applying normal holds.

If you believe that the wrapped knee brace is so large and bulky it would put his opponent at a disadvantage, the wrestler cannot compete with the brace as is. This is true even if he has a doctor's statement approving the brace. Any knee brace is your judgment call; base your judgment on the guidelines in the rules book. If the wrestler can correct the brace to your satisfaction within the allotted one and a half minutes, he may participate.

Case 11: Trying to Make Weight

You should disqualify the wrestler for wearing the plastic suit. Rubber, plastic and vinyl suits are just a few of the many items that wrestlers are prohibited from using in an attempt to lose weight. Using such aids to quickly lose weight, including sweat boxes, hot showers, whirlpools and diuretics, is illegal and unsafe and results in immediate disqualification.

Case 12: Late for Weigh-In

No, the Jamestown 119-pound wrestler shall not be allowed to weigh in. He is required to be present in the designated weigh-in area at the time established for the weigh-in.

CHAPTER 6

DEFINITIONS AND MATCH CONDUCT

In chapter 5 we looked at situations regarding the first four rules: competition, equipment, officials and their duties, and wrestlers' classifications and weigh-in. In this chapter we'll consider situations that pertain to Rules 5 and 6: Definitions and Match Conduct.

Again, these situations are just a sampling of what you might face and reflect only a portion of what you should know. Study your rules book thoroughly. If you have studied well, the following situations should be easy for you to rule on.

Rule 5: Definitions

Definitions cover a lot of territory, including positions, individual scoring maneuvers and match results. Following are a few situations that you could find yourself in. Consider how you'd rule and then check the answers beginning on page 74.

CASE 1: Pulling an Opponent Inbounds

Midway through the second period, York's 171-pound (78-kilogram) wrestler has his Jamestown opponent in a pinning situation near the edge of the mat. The Jamestown wrestler's shoulders are touching out of bounds, though the supporting parts of the York wrestler are inbounds. How much time do you allow the York wrestler to pull his opponent inbounds before you call out of bounds?

CASE 2: Escape or Takedown

The 215-pound (98-kilogram) wrestler from Pittsfield assumes his chosen offensive starting position against the opponent from Brownsburg. At the sound of your whistle, the Pittsfield wrestler releases his opponent and backs away three steps before immediately coming forward and grabbing the Brownsburg wrestler in a control situation. How do you score this? Is this an escape by the Brownsburg wrestler followed by a takedown for the Pittsfield wrestler?

CASE 3: Earning a Reversal

In the 119-pound (54-kilogram) match, the Centralia wrestler is in the offensive position. The Richmond wrestler successfully comes to his feet and executes a standing switch. He then gains control of the Centralia wrestler in a rear standing position. Has the Richmond wrestler earned a reversal?

CASE 4: Scoring a Fall or Near Fall

In the 189-pound (86-kilogram) match between Westwood and Independence, the Westwood wrestler has his opponent in a pinning situation at the edge of the mat. Only the Independence wrestler's head and shoulders are inbounds; his scapulas and the rest of his body are out of bounds. Can the Westwood wrestler score a fall or near fall in this situation?

Would your response be different if the Independence wrestler's left shoulder and scapula were inbounds but his right shoulder and scapula were out of bounds? What if his scapulas were inbounds but his head and shoulders were out of bounds? Can the Westwood wrestler score a fall or near fall in either of these situations?

Rule 6: Match Conduct

Rule 6 delineates a variety of match situations, including match length, starting the match, position choice, stopping and starting the match, end-of-match procedure, correcting errors and overtime. In this section we present a few of those situations. Make your call and then see how you did by reviewing the answers beginning on page 74 at the end of the chapter.

CASE 5: Replacing a Wrestler

Brownsburg is wrestling in a dual meet at Jamestown. Each team has weighed in two contestants for the 125-pound (57-kilogram) class. After the 119-pound (54-kilogram) match is over, one of the Brownsburg wrestlers who qualified for the 125-pound class reports to the scorer's table before the Jamestown wrestler. However, the Jamestown wrestler was required to report first. As soon as the Brownsburg coach sees who Jamestown is wrestling at 125 pounds, he recalls the wrestler who has already reported and sends up the other wrestler who qualified at 125 pounds. The Jamestown coach protests, saying a Brownsburg wrestler has already reported. Is the switch made by the Brownsburg coach legal?

CASE 6: Putting Time Back on the Clock

With 25 seconds gone in the third period of the 140-pound (64-kilogram) match between Pittsfield and Westwood, you warn the Pittsfield wrestler, who is the offensive wrestler, for stalling, but you don't stop the match. At the end of the period, the Westwood coach goes to the scorer's table and says an error has been made and should be corrected. The coach claims that the final one minute and 35 seconds, or from the point the Pittsfield wrestler was warned for stalling, should be wrestled again. What should you do?

CASE 7: An Incorrect Start

The 152-pound (69-kilogram) wrestler for York is given his choice of starting positions to begin the third period, but the choice should have gone to his Independence opponent. This error isn't detected until 30 seconds into the period, during which time the Independence wrestler is called for unsportsmanlike conduct. How do you handle this situation? Should you delete the Independence wrestler's penalty?

CASE 8: Correcting a Scoring Error

During the 171-pound (78-kilogram) match between Richmond and Brownsburg, there's a flurry of action in the first period and you correctly award the Richmond wrestler a takedown. However, the scorer inadvertently gives the two points to the Brownsburg wrestler. At the end of the first period, the Brownsburg wrestler wins the disk toss and, seeing that he is winning, decides to take the advantage position. During the second period, the Brownsburg wrestler earns a near fall and the Richmond wrestler is awarded a reversal.

As the third period begins, the Richmond coach calls the scoring error to your attention. You review the scorecard and see that the scorer has indeed made an error. You make the correction, changing the score to 4-2 in favor of the Richmond wrestler.

Neither wrestler scores in the third period and you declare the Richmond wrestler the winner. The Brownsburg coach contends that his wrestler was placed at a disadvantage and that his strategy, which was based on the incorrect score, would have been different if he had known the correct score. Do you change the outcome?

Answers

See how well you did by checking the following answers. The situations in this chapter represent only a few of the situations you might face as an official. Make sure you study Rules 5 and 6 in your rules book well.

Case 1: Pulling an Opponent Inbounds

This is a judgment call; there is no specific time allowed for pulling a wrestler back inbounds. The offensive wrestler is allowed a chance to bring the defensive wrestler back inbounds, but the question is whether the offensive wrestler—the York wrestler in this case—is making progress. If he is, you should permit the wrestling to continue as long as the York wrestler is still inbounds. If you observe that no progress is being made or the offensive wrestler is not attempting to pull the defensive wrestler back in, stop the match and restart it as if an out-of-bounds situation occurred from the starting position.

Case 2: Escape or Takedown

There was neither an escape nor a takedown. You can award an escape only when the Brownsburg wrestler faces the Pittsfield opponent after the opponent backs up. The Brownsburg wrestler has to turn around and face his opponent, or the Pittsfield wrestler has to come around in front of the Brownsburg wrestler.

Case 3: Earning a Reversal

Yes, the Richmond wrestler has earned a reversal by coming from underneath and gaining control of the Centralia wrestler. This control can take place on the mat or in a rear standing position.

Case 4: Scoring a Fall or Near Fall

In the first situation, with only the head and both shoulders inbounds, the Westwood wrestler can score points for a near fall or fall. Points for a near fall or fall can be scored if any part of both shoulders or both scapulas of the defensive wrestler are inbounds.

Based on those guidelines, the Westwood wrestler could not score a fall or near fall in the second situation, where the Independence wrestler has one shoulder and scapula out of bounds. He could score a fall or near fall in the third situation, where the Independence wrestler has both scapulas inbounds.

Case 5: Replacing a Wrestler

The switch made by the Brownsburg coach is legal. Jamestown was required to send its wrestler to the scorer's table first; once that wrestler reports, he cannot be withdrawn or replaced without being disqualified. Brownsburg has the opportunity to report a wrestler after Jamestown. Once a Brownsburg wrestler reports after his Jamestown counterpart, neither team's wrestler can be replaced.

Case 6: Putting Time Back on the Clock

The Westwood coach is correct. The final minute and a half should be considered bad time because you allowed wrestling to continue following a violation that should have resulted in stopping and restarting the match. The wrestlers should rewrestle the final one minute and 35 seconds.

Case 7: An Incorrect Start

The first 30 seconds is bad time, and the wrestlers should begin the third period again following a rest time of one minute, this time with the Independence wrestler choosing the starting position. However, the penalty for unsportsmanlike conduct should stand. The bad-time rule voids any points, penalties or injury time that occurs during that time—except for penalties for flagrant misconduct, unsportsmanlike conduct, unnecessary roughness, illegal holds and bleeding time. Everything that happened in this situation would be negated except for the unsportsmanlike-conduct penalty.

Case 8: Correcting a Scoring Error

While the Brownsburg coach might be right that his wrestler was placed at a disadvantage, you took appropriate action when you corrected the score at the beginning of the third period. Errors in recording scores must be corrected prior to the start of the subsequent period.

CHAPTER 7

INFRACTIONS, PENALTIES AND INJURIES

Infractions, penalties and injuries, as you may know, are all part of wrestling. As an official you need to know how to rule in wrestling situations that pertain to those issues. Take some time to read up on infractions, penalties and injuries under Rules 7 and 8 in your *NFHS Wrestling Rules Book,* and then check your knowledge against the cases and answers provided for you in this chapter.

Rule 7: Infractions

Infractions are any of numerous illegal maneuvers, including dangerous and illegal holds; potentially dangerous holds; technical violations; and stalling. Infractions also include the unsporting behavior of wrestlers (not during actual wrestling), coaches and other team personnel on the bench. As you gain experience as an official, you'll be able to better recognize situations when infractions might occur. Following are a few situations that you could find yourself in. Consider what you would do in these situations and then check the answers at the end of the chapter starting on page 79.

CASE 1: Slam at the Buzzer
In the 145-pound (66-kilogram) match between Jamestown and Pittsfield, the Jamestown wrestler is ahead 10-0 near the end of the match. The Jamestown wrestler lifts his opponent in the air and intentionally or unintentionally slams him to the mat just as the buzzer sounds to end the match. Does this slam have any bearing on the outcome of the match?

CASE 2: Headlocked
The York 171-pound (78-kilogram) wrestler has his Brownsburg opponent in a legal headlock near the end of the second period. He takes his

opponent to the mat, meeting the criteria for a near fall. In an attempt to avoid being pinned, the Brownsburg wrestler moves in a way that makes the headlock illegal. In the process the Brownsburg wrestler injures his ankle. How do you rule in this situation?

CASE 3: Incorrect Starting Position

In a spirited, high-scoring match near the end of the second period, the Centralia 135-pound (61-kilogram) wrestler takes his Westwood opponent down and they immediately go out of bounds. They return to the center of the mat with the Centralia wrestler in the advantage position. As the wrestling continues, the Centralia wrestler is guilty of a false start, then an incorrect starting position and then another incorrect starting position. What is the penalty sequence here? How many points would you penalize the Centralia wrestler?

Would your ruling be different if the sequence were a false start, another false start and then an incorrect starting position?

CASE 4: Intentionally Leaving the Wrestling Area

The Richmond 189-pound (86-kilogram) wrestler has nearly pinned his Independence opponent. They are at the mat's edge and you have reached a count of three for a near fall. The Independence wrestler then bridges and intentionally goes out of the wrestling area. How many points do you award the Richmond wrestler?

Rule 8: Penalties and Injuries

Rule 8 defines correct rulings in penalty and injury situations. Included in this rule are when and how to penalize wrestlers, what penalties warrant an initial warning and the consequences of being penalized, and how to proceed in injury situations. Following are a few of the situations you might find yourself in during a match; consider how you would respond and then check your answers beginning on page 80 at the end of the chapter.

CASE 5: Racking Up the Points

In the 215-pound (98-kilogram) match between Jamestown and Centralia, you penalize the Jamestown wrestler in the first period for an illegal hold. In the second period, you penalize the Jamestown wrestler for a technical violation, and later in that period you warn him about stalling. In the third period, you penalize him for unsportsmanlike conduct. How many points is the Centralia wrestler awarded based on these calls?

CASE 6: Flagrant Misconduct

The Pittsfield 119-pound (54-kilogram) wrestler pins his Westwood opponent. As the Pittsfield wrestler begins to leave the mat, he strikes the Westwood wrestler and is penalized for flagrant misconduct. What is the outcome of the match?

CASE 7: Coaching During Injury Time-Out

In the 135-pound (61-kilogram) match between York and Richmond, the York wrestler sustains a shoulder injury and asks for injury time. You grant the injury time-out. As the York wrestler goes to his corner of the mat, his shoulder is tended to and his coach also instructs him regarding the match. The Richmond coach notices this and complains that the York wrestler is being coached during an injury time-out. What's your call in this situation?

CASE 8: Unable to Continue Wrestling

In a tight match at 152 pounds (69 kilograms) between Brownsburg and Independence with the Independence wrestler leading 10-9, the Brownsburg wrestler attempts to turn the Independence wrestler with a half nelson. In doing so, the Independence wrestler injures his shoulder. The Independence wrestler is unable to continue wrestling after the injury time-out. What's the outcome of the match?

Answers

Now that you've explored each of the situations in this chapter, you can check your responses against the following answers. As an official you want to be thoroughly versed in penalties and injuries, so make sure you study Rules 7 and 8 in your *NFHS Wrestling Rules Book.*

Case 1: Slam at the Buzzer

Yes, a wrestler who has his opponent in the air is responsible for his safe return to the mat. If you deem that the slam was intentional, then it is a flagrant misconduct and you should disqualify the Jamestown wrestler and declare the Pittsfield wrestler the winner. You must call a slam immediately, without any hesitation.

If you believe the slam to be accidental, then the Pittsfield wrestler would have recovery time to determine whether he could continue wrestling. If he could continue and there was no injury (as he is not permitted to continue if he is injured), you would penalize the Jamestown wrestler for the slam and the match would conclude with the Jamestown wrestler winning, 10-1. If, however, the Pittsfield wrestler were unable to continue after two minutes of recovery time, he would be declared the winner because of the slam.

Case 2: Headlocked

The first thing that you should do is immediately stop the match as soon as you recognize the illegal headlock. You shouldn't penalize the York wrestler, because it was the Brownsburg wrestler's move that caused the headlock to become illegal. The injury has nothing to do with how you call the headlock situation. You should, of course, give the Brownsburg wrestler injury time. If the Brownsburg wrestler cannot continue after the injury time is up, you should then declare the York wrestler the victor.

Case 3: Incorrect Starting Position

The penalty sequence for a false start, incorrect starting position and another incorrect starting position is caution, caution and a one-point penalty against the Centralia wrestler. This also holds true for the other sequence as well (two false starts followed by an incorrect starting position). For any sequence involving false starts and incorrect starting positions, you issue two cautions. On the third infraction, you would apply the one-point penalty.

Case 4: Intentionally Leaving the Wrestling Area

When a wrestler goes out of the wrestling area or forces his opponent to leave the wrestling area to avoid wrestling, it is a technical violation, except in a pinning situation when near-fall points have been earned. In this case, you should award the Richmond wrestler two points for a near fall. There are no penalty points to award.

If this were not a near-fall situation, you would penalize the Independence wrestler one point for a technical violation.

Case 5: Racking Up the Points

The Centralia wrestler is awarded one point for the illegal hold in the first period, one point for the technical violation in the second period and two match points for the unsportsmanlike-conduct penalty in the third period. Had the unsportsmanlike-conduct call occurred either before the match started or after it ended, it would have resulted in a deduction of one team point from Jamestown's total.

Case 6: Flagrant Misconduct

In this situation, you would disqualify the Pittsfield wrestler and deduct two team points from Pittsfield's score because of the flagrant misconduct call. You do not award any team points. If this were to happen in tournament action, however, neither wrestler would advance in the bracket.

Case 7: Coaching During Injury Time-Out

There is no call to make. Injured wrestlers can receive coaching during an injury time-out.

Case 8: Unable to Continue Wrestling

The half nelson applied by the Brownsburg wrestler is a legal hold, and he can't be penalized for applying it. Although the Independence wrestler was ahead when the match was stopped, you should declare the Brownsburg wrestler the winner by default.

CHAPTER 8

Tournament Scoring and Conduct

The final two rules concern the scoring and conduct of tournaments. In this chapter we'll present you with situations in which you must consider these rules. Scoring, of course, is of great interest to wrestlers, coaches and fans, and misinterpretation of Rule 9 will result in great contention. As for Rule 10, tournaments are conducted differently from dual meets and you need to know what the differences are.

Rule 9: Scoring

Scoring covers a great deal of ground, including individual-match scoring (takedowns, escapes, reversals, near falls, falls); dual-meet scoring (falls, forfeits, technical falls, major decisions, decisions); advancement scoring; and team scoring in tournaments. Check your knowledge by responding to the following situations. The correct answers are at the end of the chapter starting on page 85.

CASE 1: Near-Fall Points

The 160-pound (73-kilogram) wrestler for Jamestown has his York opponent in a pinning situation. He holds the shoulders of the York wrestler within four inches of the mat for seven seconds. During this time, however, you indicate only a two-second count. How many points has the Jamestown wrestler scored?

Would your response be different if the York wrestler had one shoulder on the mat and the other shoulder at less than 45 degrees to the mat, and you had given a full five-second hand count?

CASE 2: Unsportsmanlike-Conduct Scoring

The 125-pound (57-kilogram) dual-meet match ends with the Pittsfield wrestler ahead of his Brownsburg opponent, 6-4. The Brownsburg wrestler refuses to take part in the end-of-match procedures. What is the scoring?

Would the scoring be different if the Brownsburg wrestler struck the Pittsfield wrestler and then went directly to his team bench?

CASE 3: First-Place Points

In the semifinal matches of a tournament, the winners in the 112-pound (51-kilogram) weight class are from Centralia and Richmond. However, both wrestlers are injured in their semifinal matches and told by their doctors that they cannot wrestle in the finals. How should you place these two wrestlers and how should you award team points?

CASE 4: Double Disqualification

In the 275-pound (125-kilogram) finals match of a tournament, both the Westwood wrestler and the Independence wrestler are disqualified from the match because of a double stalling call. How does this affect their teams' scores?

Rule 10: Conduct of Tournaments

Tournaments are governed differently from dual meets because they include several teams and often last more than one day. Wrestler entries and tournament brackets are unique to tournaments and are covered in Rule 10. Respond to the following situations and check your answers beginning on page 86 at the end of the chapter.

CASE 5: Late to the Mat

In a tournament meet, a second-round 112-pound (51-kilogram) match pits Jamestown against Brownsburg. However, the Jamestown wrestler is not at the mat and ready to compete at the scheduled time. How long do you wait before you make a ruling, and what is your ruling if the time allowance is exceeded?

CASE 6: Injury Default

At a tournament meet, Pittsfield's 160-pound wrestler (73-kilogram) advances to a semifinals match, where he is beaten. During the match he showed no signs of being ill or injured, but after the match he appears disoriented. The medical staff treats him for exhaustion and it appears that he will be able to wrestle in the consolation semifinals.

However, the Pittsfield wrestler doesn't report to the mat for the consolation semifinals, and no one has reported the wrestler's whereabouts or condition to the tournament staff. Because he doesn't show up for the match, the Pittsfield wrestler forfeits the consolation semifinals. However, when fifth- and sixth-place finals are called to the mat, the Pittsfield wrestler shows up and says he wants to injury-default the match. Can this wrestler be awarded sixth place by injury default?

CASE 7: Bye Versus Forfeit

The 119-pound (54-kilogram) wrestler for York receives a bye in the first round of a tournament. In the same half bracket, a Westwood wrestler is scheduled to go against a Jamestown wrestler. The Jamestown wrestler forfeits the match. In the second round, the York and Westwood wrestlers are due to match up. The York wrestler, however, fails to show up for this second-round match. Would the Westwood wrestler be given a bye to the next round, or would he be declared the winner by forfeit?

CASE 8: Injury Clock

When competing against a wrestler from Brownsburg in a tournament, the Richmond 140-pound (64-kilogram) wrestler is injured through legal action and uses one minute and five seconds of injury time. The match ends in a tie and goes into overtime.

During overtime, the Richmond wrestler is again injured through legal action. As you signal for the injury clock to start, you inform the Richmond coach that his wrestler has 25 seconds remaining on his injury time. The coach disagrees, saying his wrestler should receive the full minute and a half of injury time. Is the coach correct?

Answers

Here are the answers to the questions on tournament scoring and conduct. See how you did and continue to study your rules book to gain and maintain mastery of the rules.

Case 1: Near-Fall Points

In both situations, you should award the Jamestown wrestler a three-point near fall. You should give a hand count when feasible, but it's not a necessity in awarding a three-point near fall. It's more important that you maneuver around the wrestlers to get the best vantage point.

Case 2: Unsportsmanlike-Conduct Scoring

In the first situation, where the Brownsburg wrestler refused to take part in the end-of-match procedures, you should award Pittsfield three points for the decision and deduct one point from Brownsburg for unsportsmanlike conduct. In the second situation, where the Brownsburg wrestler struck the Pittsfield wrestler, you should award Pittsfield three points for the decision and deduct three points from Brownsburg for disqualification due to flagrant misconduct.

Case 3: First-Place Points

Neither wrestler would receive first-place points because there is no first-place finisher. Each team would receive the points for second-place finishes.

Case 4: Double Disqualification

Both wrestlers would receive second-place points. This is because they were disqualified from the match but not from the tournament. Had they been disqualified from the tournament, their teams would have received no points.

   If this situation had happened in a dual meet, neither wrestler would have earned any points for his team.

Case 5: Late to the Mat

The Jamestown wrestler has five minutes to appear at the appointed mat ready to compete. Once that five-minute period is over, the wrestler forfeits the match.

Case 6: Injury Default

No, the Pittsfield wrestler cannot be awarded sixth place by injury default. The final minute and a half should be considered bad time—time that has expired during a correctable situation—because you allowed wrestiling to continue following a violation that should have resulted in starting and restopping the match. Because nothing was mentioned to the tournament director before the wrestler's forfeit in the consolation semifinals, the Pittsfield wrestler is out of the tournament and therefore cannot receive sixth place.

Case 7: Bye Versus Forfeit

No byes can carry over into the second round, so you would declare the Westwood wrestler winner of the 119-pound match by forfeit.

Case 8: Injury Clock

The Richmond coach is wrong. Overtime is an extension of regulation time; all points, penalties, cautions, warnings, bleeding time and injury time are cumulative and carry over into overtime. Because the Richmond wrestler had already used one minute and five seconds of injury time, he has only 25 seconds remaining.

PART IV

Greco-Roman and Freestyle Wrestling

Now we're turning to something completely different—in fact, *two* things that are completely different from the folkstyle wrestling that has been our focus thus far. In part IV, we introduce you to Greco-Roman and freestyle wrestling. These styles are not used in American high schools or sanctioned by the NFHS, but they are a significant part of the wrestling world beyond high school competition. In the next three chapters, we'll look at how the styles and their rules differ from those of folkstyle, what the officials' duties are, and how competitions are conducted.

CHAPTER 9

INTRODUCTION TO GRECO-ROMAN AND FREESTYLE WRESTLING

Thus far we've covered the principles, mechanics and rules for officiating folkstyle wrestling. Now we're going to look at officiating Greco-Roman and freestyle wrestling meets.

Folkstyle is firmly entrenched in high schools, but the International Amateur Wrestling Federation recognizes more than 160 traditional variants around the world. USA Wrestling conducts national championships in folkstyle, Greco-Roman and freestyle wrestling. At the Olympics and at world championships, competitions are held in two styles: Greco-Roman and freestyle. We'll introduce you to these two styles, including background, wrestling specifics, uniform requirements, weight classifications, weigh-in procedures, coaching rules and mat regulations.

Wrestling Styles

Greco-Roman and freestyle wrestling have many more commonalities than differences.

First we'll introduce you to the styles in the order in which they originated. Then we'll move into each style's regulations.

Greco-Roman Wrestling

Modern Greco-Roman wrestling was created in France in the early 19th century based on classical Greek and Roman representations of the sport. It is especially popular in Europe, but it is also common in the rest of the world, including the United States. The rules and procedures are essentially the same as for freestyle, with one key difference: In Greco-Roman wrestling, a wrestler cannot attack his opponent's legs or use his own legs to trip, lift or execute moves. The wrestler must wrestle from a standing position without the top of his head touching his opponent's chest, and he can take no holds below the waist. The wrestler must accompany his opponent to the mat in order to score points. Additionally, a wrestler who continually avoids contact is fleeing the hold, which results in a caution and one point awarded to the opponent. (We will cover prohibitions and other rules more fully in chapter 11.)

Freestyle Wrestling

Freestyle is the most popular wrestling style in the world and its participants include both men and women. It appeared at the Olympic Games in 1904, and the first freestyle world championship took place in Helsinki in 1951. Though the ancient Greeks trained young women in wrestling, women were not allowed to take part in the ancient Olympic Games. Women's wrestling only became recognized as a sport in recent years. Women's world championships have been held since the 1980s, and an increasing number of countries enter these championships each year. It became an Olympic sport in 2004. Women's freestyle wrestling is growing in popularity in the United States and around the world.

Freestyle is similar to folkstyle but uses different scoring and strategies. Its rules and procedures are similar to those of Greco-Roman wrestling with the exception of leg usage—in freestyle, wrestlers can use their arms and legs to attack, execute holds and defend against attacks. The use of the legs is an integral part of freestyle wrestling, just as it is in folkstyle wrestling. As in Greco-Roman wrestling, a wrestler who constantly avoids contact can be called for fleeing a hold. The rules for women are the same as for men, with a few modifications, such as, for example, in women's wrestling, all double nelsons are illegal.

Wrestler Regulations

Wrestlers must adhere to various regulations pertaining to their uniforms, weight classes and weigh-ins. As you read about these regulations, note the differences from folkstyle regulations. If you're used to officiating at folkstyle competitions and are moving into Greco-Roman and freestyle wrestling, you'll need to familiarize yourself thoroughly with the different regulations.

Uniforms

For national and international competitions, wrestlers wear a one-piece singlet, one wrestler wearing red, the other blue. In folkstyle, wrestlers also wear a singlet, but they aren't restricted to red or blue. For local events, other colors can be approved. Leggings are not allowed in freestyle wrestling.

Wrestlers must carry a handkerchief or paper towel. They use the handkerchief to wipe off bodily fluids such as blood and spittle. Wrestlers carry the handkerchief inside their singlets. The handkerchief is to be present to the referee when the wrestler reports to the center of the mat.

Except in cases of injury or doctor's orders (wrestler must present a doctor's note to the official), wrestlers cannot wear bandages on their wrists, arms or ankles. When bandaging is allowed, it must be covered by elastic strapping. Wrestlers also cannot have any greasy or sticky substance on their bodies. They must be clean-shaven at the beginning of the competition day or have a beard of several months' growth, which also applies to hair on the head. It is suggested that women or other wrestlers with long hair have the hair fixed in a manner that will not cause any delay in wrestling. Additionally, they cannot wear objects such as rings or earrings that might injure their opponent.

Weight Classes

The weight classes for Greco-Roman and freestyle wrestling differ from folkstyle classes. Again, if you're used to officiating at folkstyle events, make sure you're using the correct weight classes at weigh-ins for Greco-Roman and freestyle wrestling.

The international weight divisions for Seniors in Greco-Roman and freestyle wrestling are as follows:

Men's Weight Classes
- 50-55 kg (110-121 lbs)
- 60 kg (132 lbs)
- 66 kg (145.5 lbs)
- 74 kg (163 lbs)
- 84 kg (185 lbs)
- 96 kg (212 lbs)
- 120 kg (264.5 lbs)

Women's Weight Classes
- 48 kg (106 lbs)
- 51 kg (112 lbs)
- 55 kg (121 lbs)
- 59 kg (130 lbs)
- 63 kg (139 lbs)
- 67 kg (148 lbs)
- 72 kg (159 lbs)

Note that weight classifications can change depending on the governing body and competition. In men's wrestling, USA Wrestling has 10 weight categories for Schoolboys (ages 13 to 15), 17 for Cadets (ages 15 to 17), 15 for Juniors (ages 18 to 20) and 7 for Seniors (20 and older, though Juniors can also wrestle in Senior competitions). In women's wrestling, USA Wrestling has 10 categories for Schoolgirls (ages 13 to 15), 11 for Cadets (ages 15 to 17), 9 for Juniors (ages 18 to 20) and 7 for Seniors (20 and older, though girls who are age 17 or older in the year of the event can wrestle at the Senior level).

Weigh-In Procedures

Wrestlers weigh in before competition and must be at or below a weight level to be able to wrestle. In folkstyle, the weigh-in takes place a maximum of one hour before duals and two hours before tournaments. For Greco-Roman or freestyle meets, the weigh-in is generally a maximum of three, and a minimum of two, hours before competition. In multiday competition, wrestlers must weigh in each day before they compete.

Wrestlers are weighed with only an approved singlet on, and socks and shoes are not necessary. Wrestlers, whether male or female, can be weighed in by a person of either gender. Wrestlers are allowed to step on the scale one time and if they don't make weight, they can request a weigh-in on another scale. This weigh-in must take place immediately without the wrestler leaving the weigh-in area.

Additionally, wrestlers should be present at the weigh-in, having already been examined by a doctor to determine whether they have any contagious diseases. Any wrestler with such a disease cannot compete.

Coaches

Coaches must be at least two meters (7 feet) from the outside edge of the passivity zone during competition. At USA Wrestling events two coaches per wrestler are allowed in this area, but at international events—those held under Fédération Internationnal de Lutte Amateur (FILA) rules without modification—only one coach is allowed.

Coaches can talk only to their wrestlers. Coaches cannot attempt to influence the officials by shouting out how many points they believe a wrestler just earned or by making any other calls (illegal holds, other penalties, passivity and so on). If a coach has a question, he may approach the mat chairman and request a meeting. In this meeting, the coach quickly verbalizes his concerns, is given an explanation and then returns to his chair.

Coaches who verbally abuse an official or otherwise break the rules receive a yellow card for the first offense, meaning they must leave the mat area, and a red card for the second offense, meaning they must leave the event facility.

Mat

The mat has a 9-meter (30 feet) circular competition area, with a 1.2- to 1.5-meter (4-5 feet) protection border (see figure 9.1). This is similar to the folkstyle mat, which is a minimum of 28 feet in diameter with a safety area about 5 feet wide.

There is a 1-meter (3 feet) passivity zone on the inside of the edge of the 9-meter circle. This is close to the edge of the mat. When wrestlers approach this area, you should encourage them to stay within the competition area. Verbalize either "blue zone" or "red zone" and point to the zone with the entire hand of the correct color.

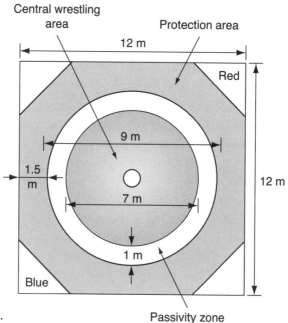

FIGURE 9.1
Regulation Greco-Roman and freestyle wrestling mat.

Total Wrestling

To keep the sport invigorating and exciting, the concept of total wrestling has come to the forefront in recent years. Total wrestling puts a premium on constant activity, aggression and taking risks. To score, the wrestlers must take risks; if they become passive they will be penalized. Bouts have been shortened to facilitate this active, aggressive style of wrestling. The most successful wrestlers are those who have prepared for and adopted this total-wrestling style.

Officiating at Greco-Roman or Freestyle Events

So what does all this mean for you as an official? If you officiate Greco-Roman or freestyle competitions, you of course need to know your duties and responsibilities, which we cover in the next chapter. Also, you need to know the rules and regulations of these wrestling styles. For complete rules, get a copy of USA Wrestling's *International Rule Book and Guide to Wrestling: Freestyle, Greco-Roman and Women's*.

Following are some of the essential differences between Greco-Roman and freestyle and folkstyle, which is most commonly used in high school wrestling:

- In Greco-Roman and freestyle, very little emphasis is placed on control; folkstyle places great emphasis on control.

- In Greco-Roman and freestyle, wrestlers are brought to their feet after a short period of time if no scoring occurs.

- In Greco-Roman and freestyle, wrestlers can score without having control of their opponent. Moves such as tilts, front headlocks from the knees and crotch lifts while under attack can score without the wrestler ever gaining control. Scoring occurs when a wrestler exposes his opponent's back.

- In Greco-Roman and freestyle, wrestlers are not penalized for attempting a throw if they can make it to their knees (with their stomach facing the mat) after a failed attempt. Getting to their knees is not as important as facing the mat, belly down. This is called a slip, and wrestling continues after a slip with no points scored for the wrestler on top. In order to score, the wrestler being attacked must take the move away by reversing direction or preventing the opponent from making it to his knees.

As with the wrestling itself, there are more similarities than differences in officiating a Greco-Roman or freestyle match and a folkstyle match. In the next chapter we'll look at your specific duties for officiating Greco-Roman and freestyle matches.

CHAPTER 10

Officials' Duties

As an official of Greco-Roman and freestyle wrestling, your duties and responsibilities are largely the same as for folkstyle wrestling. However, there are some differences. Those differences are the focus of this chapter.

General Duties

In USA Wrestling events, ideally there are three officials—a mat chairman, a referee and a judge—but in most events, all three are not required. When three officials do work together, the referee and judge work under the direction of the mat chairman. Each official evaluates the holds and moves of the wrestlers, with the judge and the mat chairman recording points on individual scorecards. Following are the duties of each of the three officials.

Uniform Requirements

For most USA Wrestling competitions, officials wear a blue polo shirt, gray pants, black belt and black athletic shoes. For Amateur Athletic Union wrestling, officials wear a white shirt or pullover, white pants and shoes. Check with your governing body for the proper uniform.

Officials also wear a red armband on the left arm and a blue armband on the right arm. When a wrestler scores one or more points, the official raises the appropriate arm—left arm for the red wrestler, right arm for the blue wrestler—and indicates how many points were scored with the fingers of the raised hand. Greco-Roman and freestyle use the thumb for one point and the thumb and consecutive fingers for more than one point.

Referee

As referee, you are responsible for the orderly conduct of the bout. You will work closely with the judge. Your whistle begins, interrupts and ends the bout. It is also your responsibility to keep the action flowing. Make sure that you intervene only when appropriate, that is, to warn wrestlers for passivity, penalize them for illegal holds, move them back onto the mat when they stray from the wrestling area and so on.

You need to be active and alert on the mat, ready to change your position from one moment to the next, always angling to get the best view. If a fall appears imminent, you should lower yourself, watching the shoulders of the wrestler who is in danger of being pinned. In this way you can be in the best position to observe a pin without obstructing the view of the judges or the public.

When wrestlers are standing, make sure you are not too close to them. This is especially important in Greco-Roman wrestling, where you need to be able to see their legs. If, however, the wrestlers are in par terre position (on the ground; this position is described more fully in the next chapter), you can move in closer to observe their holds and stop dangerous or illegal actions before injury occurs.

Wrestling is set up to reward active and aggressive wrestlers and dissuade passivity. With this in mind, watch for wrestlers who want to rest during the bout—to wipe their bodies, blow their noses, attend to minor (or nonexistent) injuries and so on. If you believe that a wrestler is passive in such a manner, give the offending wrestler a passivity penalty and give choice of position to the other.

Watch for passivity. You can direct the competitors to wrestle actively right away and if they continue in a state of passivity, warnings can follow. At times you can position yourself so that a passive wrestler can't leave the mat, which can prompt the action to pick up without you having to stop the bout. Also, use zone commands to indicate to the wrestlers that they need to move toward the center of the mat. Look for ways such as these to stimulate action without stopping the bout.

In Greco-Roman wrestling you must pay special attention to the legs of the wrestlers, making sure they aren't using their legs to execute moves and they aren't attacking their opponent's legs.

As a referee of Greco-Roman and freestyle wrestling, be sure to

- indicate whether a hold executed at the edge of the mat is within bounds,
- visibly count five seconds when a wrestler is in a bridge position, and

- signal and call out "Tombé" (fall; pronounced "tom-BAY") when a wrestler's shoulders are pinned to the mat for one second. When this happens, look for confirmation from your judge or mat chairman and when you have it, strike the mat with your hand and then blow your whistle.

Finally, if a wrestler is ahead by 10 points, according to USA Wrestling, he is the winner on technical superiority. At this point, once any current action is completed (i.e., an attack or counterattack) you should stop the bout and ask the winning wrestler if he wants to continue the bout. If the wrestler chooses to end the bout, the bout is over. If the wrestler wants to continue, the bout goes on until regulation time is over or a fall is awarded. Some organizations automatically end the bout once technical superiority is achieved.

Judge

As judge, you must indicate your opinion on each action, using your hand or paddles and record points on a scorecard. In addition, you verify falls and passivity.

It's your duty to call to the referee's attention anything that appears irregular that he did not catch. You also have a set of paddles in different colors that represent each point value (1, 2, 3 and 5), and you have a plain paddle for passivities and cautions and a white paddle for indicating no score or that the judge or chairman do not agree with the referee's call.

At the end of a bout, you sign your scorecard, crossing out the name of the losing wrestler and circling the name of the winner. In addition, there are several other things you must do:

- Underline the points received by a wrestler for executing a gut wrench.
- Note a wrestler who received a caution for brutality, fleeing the mat, fleeing the hold, executing an illegal hold or assuming an incorrect position by placing an "O" in the column of the offending wrestler.
- Indicate the wrestler who had the hold first in a clinch situation by placing a "K" in the appropriate column, and box in the points scored from the clinch.

Mat Chairman

As mat chairman, you are responsible for coordinating the work of the referee and judge. In case of disagreement between the referee and judge, you make the final decision. You give your opinion only if the referee and judge disagree.

In USA Wrestling events for Junior, Cadet and Kids divisions, the mat chairman can call a conference if an error has been made, even if the judge and referee agree on what transpired on the mat. At these levels it is the mat chairman's duty to make sure that the rules have been correctly applied.

The mat chairman's scorecard is the official scorecard. If there is a discrepancy among the officials' scorecards, the mat chairman's scorecard is final.

Now that we've considered general duties, in the next chapter we'll look at the specifics of officiating Greco-Roman and freestyle wrestling.

CHAPTER 11

COMPETITION

In this chapter we'll examine basic rules and procedures for a bout, and we'll define positions, holds and penalties that you will need to know as an official of Greco-Roman and freestyle wrestling. Finally, we'll look at scoring and winning a bout.

Much of the information in this chapter comes from USA Wrestling's *International Rule Book and Guide to Wrestling: Freestyle, Greco-Roman and Women's, 2003 Edition.* For more detailed information, refer to this resource.

Bout Basics

Every wrestler's main objective, of course, is to win the bout. A victory is most decisively achieved by pinning the opponent (holding the shoulder blades—or entire surface of the scapula—to the mat for half a second). Barring a pin, a wrestler wins on points. We'll explore how points are scored later in this chapter.

Bout Length

Bout length depends on the age group and the sanctioning organization. Following are some common lengths, but be sure to check with the organization governing the event.

- *Schoolboy and Schoolgirl, Cadet (ages 13-15, 15-17).* Two periods of two minutes each with 30 seconds of rest in between. Overtime is two minutes.
- *Junior, Senior (ages 18-20, 20 and older).* For men, two periods of three minutes each with 30 seconds of rest in between and overtime is three minutes. For women, three periods of two minutes each with 30 seconds of rest in between and overtime is three minutes.
- *Veterans (35 and older).* Three periods of two minutes each with 30 seconds of rest in between. Overtime is two minutes.

If the score is tied at the end of regulation or if neither wrestler has scored at least three points, the bout goes into overtime. For Seniors, there is no rest period and wrestling begins immediately for the prescribed length of time or until the first technical point is scored, if this puts the winner's total to at least three points.

The overtime period begins in the standing position. If the score is still tied at the end of the overtime period, the officiating team decides the winner. The criteria is based on the number of cautions and passivities for each wrestler. If these are tied, each official must cast a vote for the most aggressive wrestler.

Starting the Bout

As wrestlers report to the mat, you should check them for long fingernails, wet or greasy skin, hair or skin infections, and missing handkerchiefs. The wrestlers shake hands with you and with each other, and on your whistle the match begins with both wrestlers standing.

If no points have been scored after approximately 45 to 60 seconds, you should call the less aggressive wrestler for passivity and give the choice of position to the other wrestler. If there is no clear aggressor, assign passivities equally to one wrestler and then the other, spacing the calls evenly throughout the first period.

Interrupting the Bout

There are several situations in which you should interrupt a bout. These situations have to do with the wrestlers' position on the mat, passivity, injuries and serious errors. You will not always interrupt the bout in these situations; circumstances dictate whether you step in. In this section we'll look at when and when not to interrupt a bout, how to interrupt it, and how the bout should proceed from there.

Position on the Mat   Stop the wrestlers if one foot of either wrestler touches outside the passivity zone (see figure 11.1). You should also stop them if they remain in the passivity zone (at least three of the four feet are in the zone) and neither wrestler is able to execute a hold (see figure 11.2). In both cases, resume the wrestling at the center of the mat with the wrestlers standing.

However, do let the match continue if the wrestler with his back to the out-of-bounds area (the protection area) is under attack. When the attack is over (inbounds or out), stop the bout and award the appropriate points for the action. Only the attacking wrestler may score points. If, however, during a front headlock (from the feet or mat) that starts inbounds, the attacker touches both shoulders and finishes the attack out of bounds,

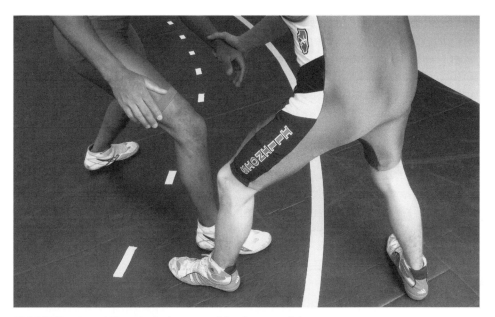

FIGURE 11.1   Wrestler's foot outside the passivity zone.

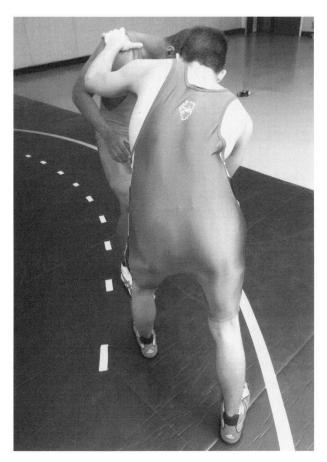

FIGURE 11.2   Wrestlers remaining in the passivity zone.

it would be scored three or two points for the attacker and two for the defender, even if the defender did nothing.

In par terre wrestling, as discussed further in "Par Terre Position," the pinning points (shoulders) of the defensive wrestler determine inbounds unless the head touches out of bounds, in which case the wrestlers are out. Wrestling continues as long as an attack is taking place.

Passivity   When you observe a wrestler being passive, without stopping the bout you should tell the wrestler to be more active. If the wrestler remains passive, you should raise your arm with the armband signifying the passive wrestler and announce passivity. After the judge or mat chairman shows agreement with your call, you should stop the bout, warn the wrestler for passivity and ask the passive wrestler's opponent if he wants to resume the bout standing or par terre. You can give this passivity warning an unlimited number of times. For more on passivity, see page 104.

Injuries   If a wrestler is injured, you should stop the bout and the team's medical personnel should tend to the wrestler on the mat. If the injury is severe and requires that the wrestler be removed for treatment elsewhere, that of course is allowed.

When a wrestler is injured, there is no time limit on the treatment, although the two-minute rule is in effect at competitions where there are no doctors. In that case the wrestler must be ready to wrestle within two minutes. Blood time, similar to injury time, may also be called when blood is present but is kept separately and is five minutes in duration. During the break coaches can advise their wrestlers. The timer calls out each 30 seconds of this two-minute period, and when 10 seconds remain you call the wrestlers to the center of the mat to resume the bout.

If a bout must be stopped for medical reasons, the medical personnel inform the coach as well as the mat chairman, who then orders the bout to be stopped.

Serious Errors   The mat chairman can ask the referee to stop the bout if a serious error has occurred. The officials will then consult with each other and correct the error before continuing the bout.

If a bout has to be stopped because one wrestler has deliberately injured the other, the wrestler who caused the injury is disqualified and the injured wrestler is the winner. If it is a tournament bout, the offending wrestler risks being disqualified from the tournament as well, which is based on the agreement of all three officials.

When a wrestler has taken his opponent to the mat, he has the option of wrestling in the par terre position, which literally means "on the ground" (see figure 11.3). In par terre, the wrestler on top attempts to turn his opponent's shoulders past 90 degrees, putting the opponent in a danger position, or a position where he could get pinned (see figure 11.4). If no action is taking place and it's obvious that the attacking wrestler is not going to succeed, return the wrestlers to the standing position. A wrestler doesn't score points for controlling his opponent in the par terre position.

FIGURE 11.3   Wrestlers in the par terre position.

FIGURE 11.4   Wrestler putting his opponent in a danger position.

The wrestler underneath tries to counter his opponent's efforts and get to a standing position or counterattack. The wrestler on top must remain active. If he is warned for passivity, his opponent has the choice of resuming the par terre position, this time starting on top. The wrestler on top may not request to stop the bout and restart it from a standing position.

Finally, if the wrestlers leave the mat while in the par terre position, they stop and then resume the bout in the same position.

Ending the Bout

A bout can end in various ways. As a referee, you need to know the ways a bout can end and the procedures that follow the end of a bout.

A bout ends when any of these situations occur:

- A wrestler pins the opponent
- A wrestler gets ahead by 10 or more points (technical superiority)
- A wrestler is disqualified
- A wrestler is injured and unable to continue
- Regulation time expires with the wrestler who is ahead in points having scored at least three points
- Overtime expires

Signal the end of regulation or overtime by blowing your whistle once the timer indicates (usually with a gong) that time has expired. Any action begun by a wrestler at the sound of the gong does not count.

After ending the bout, stand in the center of the mat, facing the officials' table. The wrestlers stand on either side of you, awaiting the decision. They shake hands while waiting. When the decision is announced, raise the hand of the victor. The wrestlers shake hands with you, the opposing coach and each of the members of the officiating team.

Passivity

Passivity goes directly against the concept of total wrestling, in which activity and aggressiveness are prized. When a wrestler is passive, he is merely holding ground and trying to neutralize his opponent; he is not aggressively attacking his opponent and attempting holds. Other signs of passivity include continually obstructing the opponent's holds, holding the opponent by one or both hands to prevent him from wrestling, continually lying stomach-down without counterattacking, fleeing the mat or pushing the opponent off the mat, and deliberately falling to the ground. In freestyle, a passive wrestler might grip one leg of the opponent between his own legs while remaining flat on his stomach. In Greco-Roman, a passive tactic is to engage the opponent with the head thrust forward, thus preventing body-to-body contact.

Watch for these and other signs of passivity and communicate to passive wrestlers that they must initiate action. If the passive wrestler does not become active after your command, stop the bout and issue a warning. Then restart the bout, giving the opponent the choice of starting while standing or in the par terre position.

Be careful when issuing warnings; give wrestlers enough time, especially in the par terre position, to initiate holds. Never interrupt a hold as it is being executed.

Passivity Zone and Protection Area

The passivity zone (see area noted on figure 9.1 on page 93) helps you detect passive wrestlers. Such wrestlers tend to move toward this zone, moving farther and farther away from the center in an attempt to flee their opponent. The moment a wrestler places a foot in the passivity zone, you should call out "Zone!" in a loud voice. The wrestlers must then attempt to move back toward the center of the mat without interrupting their action.

All holds that begin in the center and end in the passivity zone are valid. Action can continue in the passivity zone as long as execution of the holds is not interrupted. A wrestler can even move his opponent farther into the passivity zone if the action is continuous. While wrestling in the par terre position, any action, hold or counterattack in the passivity zone is good, even if it ends in the protection area. However, if one foot of the attacking wrestler is in the protection area, stop the bout and resume it in the center of the mat. The exception to this is when a wrestler moves out of the zone as he is attacking. In that case all four legs of the wrestlers can be off the mat if the shoulders and head of the defending wrestler are within the zone.

Once the action abates or two, three or four of the wrestlers' feet are in the zone, interrupt the bout and bring the wrestlers back to the central area. You don't need to issue warnings for passivity.

If a hold ends in the protection area, stop the wrestling and resume it in a par terre position at the center of the mat. You should award points for holds that end in the protection area as long as the holds originate elsewhere on the mat. If the defending wrestler places a foot in the protection area while the attacking wrestler is executing a hold and is continuously active, the hold is valid.

A fall in the protection area—which is the area of the mat between the outside edge of the passivity zone and the floor—however, is not valid. In fact, if a wrestler executes a hold and arrives in a fall position in the protection area, his opponent receives two points. Again, you would return the wrestlers to the center of the mat and resume the match in the par terre position.

Clinch

The clinch rule, where wrestlers start in some form of contact, is intended to fight passivity. It's a somewhat controversial rule that is guaranteed to produce scoring. The clinch rule is instituted at the beginning of the second period if the score is 0-0 and at the beginning of overtime if neither wrestler has scored three or more points. You can also order a clinch in the second period and in overtime if one wrestler is cautioned twice for passivity and no points have been scored during that period (other than any points scored from a clinch to start the period).

After a scoreless first period, the winner of a disc toss clinches first. At the start of overtime, the wrestler with the fewest cautions for passivity clinches first. A wrestler clinches his opponent by wrapping his arms around the opponent in a chest-to-chest hold in a standing position. One arm is under an arm of the opponent; the other arm is outside the opponent's arm (see figure 11.5). The wrestler executing the clinch can choose which arm to place under the arm of his opponent. Once the wrestlers are in position, blow your whistle to begin the action.

If the wrestler applying the clinch doesn't score within one minute, the opponent is awarded a point. If the wrestler applying the clinch lets go without scoring, his opponent is awarded a point. If, however, the wrestler lets go of the clinch and either of the wrestlers executes a hold as a continuation of the action, the points scored through the hold are good and the wrestler letting go of the clinch is not penalized. If one wrestler steps outside the circle, the other is given a point. If either wrestler doesn't

FIGURE 11.5   Wrestlers in a clinch position.

comply with your directions to properly set up a clinch, his opponent is given two points.

Penalties and Illegal Holds

You need to be familiar with a number of prohibitions, illegal holds and resulting penalties. First we'll look at general prohibitions and illegal holds, and then we'll look at those specific to Greco-Roman wrestling.

General Prohibitions

Wrestlers cannot pull hair, pinch skin, bite, twist fingers or do anything else with the intent of torturing the opponent. Other prohibited acts include kicking, head butting, strangling, pushing and applying holds that could cause injury. In addition, wrestlers cannot thrust an elbow or knee into their opponent's abdomen, hold the opponent by the singlet, cling to or grasp the mat, or seize the sole of the opponent's foot. (They can, however, seize the upper part of the foot or the heel.)

Illegal Holds

Illegal holds can cause serious injury and have no place in wrestling. In this section we'll discuss illegal holds and your response to them. Your response depends on whether the hold was executed by the attacking wrestler or the defending wrestler, and whether that wrestler has been cautioned for the hold.

Illegal holds include the following:

- Applying throat holds (see figure 11.6a)
- Twisting an arm beyond 90 degrees
- Applying an arm lock to the forearm (see figure 11.6b)
- Holding the head or neck with two hands (see figure 11.6c)
- Applying double nelsons that aren't executed from the side without using the legs on any part of the opponent's body (see figure 11.6d)
- Bringing the opponent's arm behind his back and twisting it so that the forearm forms an acute angle (see figure 11.6e)
- Executing a hold that stretches the opponent's spinal column (see figure 11.6f)
- Executing a chancery hold in any direction
- Using a scissor lock on the head, neck or body (see figure 11.6g)

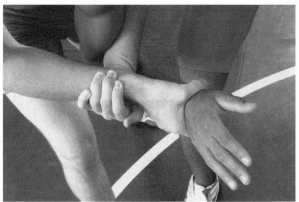

a

b

c

d

e

f

FIGURE 11.6 *(a-g)*
Illegal holds.

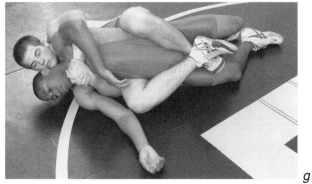

g

Wrestlers who are 13 to 17 years old have two other prohibitions that protect their health: They cannot execute double nelsons from the front or the side, and in freestyle wrestling they cannot hook an opponent's leg (see figure 11.7).

For all wrestlers, when an opponent is turned upside down in a hold from behind (in other words, a reverse waist hold), some part of the attacking wrestler's body other than his feet must touch the mat before the upper body of the attacked wrestler touches it. The fall in such a hold must not be from top to bottom—a header—but to the side.

When a wrestler is in a bridge position (see figure 11.8), it is illegal to lift him and throw him onto the mat; he must be forced out of the bridge first. Breaking a bridge by pushing in the direction of the head is also illegal.

If the attacking wrestler commits one of these violations, the action is void and the wrestler is given a caution or warning. If the attacker repeats the violation, he is given a warning and one point is awarded to the opponent, who is then given the choice of

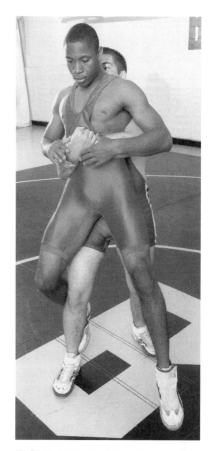

FIGURE 11.7   Wrestler executing an illegal leg hook.

FIGURE 11.8   Wrestler in a bridge position.

position. If the defending wrestler commits one of these violations, the defender is cautioned and his opponent receives two points and choice of position.

If the wrestler applying an illegal hold finds himself at a disadvantage, you should let the bout continue until the disadvantage no longer exists. Then you should stop the bout, award the appropriate points, warn the wrestler at fault and ask the other wrestler in which position he would like to resume.

If the hold is legal to begin with but then becomes illegal, stop the match and continue it in the standing position after letting the offending wrestler know that the hold became illegal. If the wrestler applies the same illegal hold, warn the wrestler, award a point to his opponent and give his opponent the choice of position.

Regardless of the circumstances, stop the action and force the wrestler to release his hold if it is dangerous. Head butting or any other form of brutality should result in immediate elimination.

Fleeing

A wrestler flees a hold when he refuses contact to prevent his opponent from executing or initiating a hold. This can happen either in the standing position or the par terre position, and it can happen anywhere on the mat. The penalty for fleeing a hold is a caution for the wrestler at fault and a point for his opponent, who is given the choice of position.

Similarly, when a wrestler flees the mat, issue a caution and give a point to the opponent plus choice of position to the opponent. When a wrestler flees the mat while in a position of danger, award the opponent two points. (A position of danger occurs when the line of a wrestler's back or shoulders forms an angle of less than 90 degrees to the mat. It also occurs when a wrestler resists with the upper part of the body to avoid a fall.) All points for fleeing the mat are technical points.

Greco-Roman Prohibitions

In Greco-Roman wrestling, when a wrestler who is on the ground jumps forward to prevent being caught in a hold and in the process puts his opponent in the position of making an illegal hold, the wrestler is fleeing the hold. The first time this happens, you should warn the wrestler. The second time, caution the wrestler and award one point to his opponent, giving the opponent choice of position. However, it is okay to move laterally while on the ground; this isn't considered fleeing the hold.

A wrestler on the ground cannot bend or raise his legs to prevent a hold. If he uses his legs as a defense, caution him and award his opponent two points.

Remember that in Greco-Roman wrestling, wrestlers cannot grab their opponents below the hips or squeeze them with their legs. Also, unlike freestyle, in Greco-Roman wrestlers must accompany their opponent to the ground.

Scoring

You need to know not only the point values of various moves and holds but also how to assess the action, when to award points and how to record points. In this section we'll look at these and other aspects of scoring.

Point Values

Wrestlers can be awarded one, two, three or five points, depending on the move, hold and circumstance. Following is an overview of how many points are awarded for various actions and holds.

One Point

- Executing a takedown (bringing the opponent to the mat from a standing position)
- Applying a correct hold while standing or par terre but not placing the opponent in danger
- Executing a reversal (when the wrestler underneath completely reverses his position and gains control on top, he has scored a reversal)
- Blocking the opponent on one or two outstretched arms with his back facing the mat (see figure 11.9)

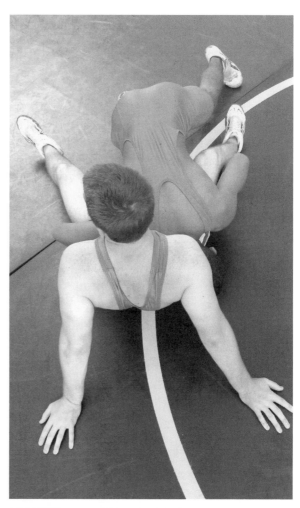

FIGURE 11.9   Wrestler blocking an opponent.

- Having the opponent flee the mat or the hold, refuse to start, commit an illegal act, or break a clinch
- Holding the opponent in a position of danger for five seconds or longer
- Executing an escape (when a wrestler breaks the control of his opponent, coming out from the bottom to face his opponent on his feet, he has scored an escape; an escape can only be earned if the top wrestler is actively trying to keep the bottom wrestler down)
- Lifting the opponent completely off the mat during a continuous hold (the wrestler is also awarded for the hold; this is an additional point for lifting the opponent off the mat)
- Exposing the opponent's shoulders to the mat

Two Points

- Applying a correct hold while in the par terre position and placing the opponent in a position of danger
- Initiating action in which the opponent rolls onto his shoulders
- Having the opponent flee the hold in a position of danger by jumping off the mat
- Being illegally held by the opponent, preventing completion of a hold the wrestler had already begun
- Causing the attacking wrestler to go into an instantaneous fall position (see figure 11.10) or roll onto the shoulders in executing a hold

FIGURE 11.10   Wrestler in an instantaneous fall position.

- Blocking the opponent while executing a hold in the standing position and in a danger position
- Having the opponent regularly refuse to take a clinch
- Exposing the opponent's shoulders to the mat and holding the opponent in a danger position for five seconds

Three Points

- Executing a hold in the standing position and bringing the opponent into a danger position through direct projection over a short amplitude (see figure 11.11)

FIGURE 11.11   Wrestler bringing his opponent into a danger position through direct projection over a short amplitude.

- Executing a hold by raising the opponent off the ground over a short amplitude, if the attack results in an immediate danger position (this can be the case even if the attacking wrestler has both knees on the ground; it can also be the case if the defending wrestler maintains contact with the mat with one hand, as long as he is placed in immediate danger)
- Executing a grand amplitude hold that does not place the opponent in an immediate danger position

Five Points

- Executing a grand amplitude hold in a standing position that puts the opponent in an immediate danger position (see figure 11.12)

FIGURE 11.12   Wrestler executing a grand amplitude hold.

- Executing a grand amplitude hold in par terre position that puts the opponent in an immediate danger position

Evaluating the Action or Hold

You will be continuously evaluating the action and holds to determine when you should award points. Just as the sport requires wrestlers to be active and aggressive, it requires officials to be knowledgeable, alert and always moving to the best position to judge the action. Make sure you wait until the end of each active situation before assessing and awarding points, and remember to award points for all actions in a series of moves, not just the final action.

Wrestlers who unsuccessfully try to execute a hold and find themselves underneath in the par terre position as a result are not penalized for their failed attempt—that is, the opponent does not receive a point for attaining the top position. The defending wrestler is only awarded points if he brings the attacking wrestler to the ground by his own continuous action and succeeds in controlling his opponent.

Examples of holds you will be evaluating are the ankle lace, the gut wrench and the grand amplitude.

Ankle Lace   An ankle lace hold (see figure 11.13) is worth one point, two points if the opponent ends in the danger position. After carrying out the hold, the wrestler must completely let go to avoid injuring the opponent.

FIGURE 11.13   Wrestler executing an ankle lace hold.

Gut Wrench   As with the ankle lace hold, a gut wrench hold (see figure 11.14) is worth two points in the danger position and one point otherwise. A wrestler who scores on a gut wrench hold must score in another manner before scoring on a gut wrench again. It is legal for a wrestler to execute several gut wrench holds in a row.

FIGURE 11.14   Wrestler executing a gut wrench hold.

Grand Amplitude   A grand amplitude hold (see figure 11.12 on page 114) occurs when a wrestler in the standing position lifts the opponent in a high, sweeping arc completely off the mat, controls him and brings him to the ground in an immediate position of danger. Such a hold is worth three points if the attacking wrestler puts the opponent on his stomach and five points if he puts the opponent in a danger position.

If the wrestler executing the grand amplitude hold touches both of his own shoulders to the mat as he executes the hold, he still receives whatever points he earned, but his opponent also receives two points because of the instantaneous fall.

Recording Points

When a fall occurs at the end of regulation, the sound of the gong determines whether the fall counts. Any hold or action is valid if it was completed before the sound of the gong. When opinions differ among officials, the mat chairman has the final decision.

The judge marks down each scoring hold and action as they occur. He circles an action bringing about a fall. Other scorecard notations include the following:

- Underlining the points for gut wrenches
- Noting cautions for fleeing the mat or a hold, refusing to start, an illegal hold and brutality with an "O" (with each caution, the opponent receives one or two points depending on the seriousness of the offense)
- Noting warnings for passivity with a "P"
- Noting the wrestler who takes a clinch with a "K"

Danger Position

We have mentioned the danger position many times in this chapter. We have described it as when the line of a wrestler's back or shoulders forms an angle of less than 90 degrees to the mat (see figure 11.15).

However, if the angle is at 90 degrees, the wrestler is not in a danger position. The danger position also doesn't exist if a wrestler exceeds the 90-degree vertical line with his chest and belly facing the mat.

The danger position occurs when

- the defending wrestler uses a bridge position to avoid being pinned,
- the defending wrestler supports himself on one or both elbows to keep his shoulders from going to the mat,

FIGURE 11.15   Wrestler in a danger position.

- a wrestler with one shoulder on the mat exceeds the 90-degree vertical line with the other shoulder,
- a wrestler is in an instantaneous fall position (he is on both shoulders
  for less than one second) or
- a wrestler rolls over onto his shoulders.

Winning the Bout

To win, a wrestler must be ahead at the end of regulation and have scored
at least three points. If the score is tied or no one has scored three points,
the bout goes into overtime. If either wrestler goes ahead and has scored
at least three points in the overtime period, the bout ends immediately. If
neither wrestler qualifies for a win by the end of overtime, the wrestler
with more technical points wins. If the match is still tied, the wrestler
with the fewest cautions and warnings for passivity wins. If the wrestlers
have the same total number of cautions and warnings, the one with the
fewest warnings wins. If these marks are still equal, the officials choose
the winner.

Wrestlers can achieve victory by pinning the opponent (holding
both shoulders to the mat while in control of the opponent as you say
"Tombé"). The shoulders must be completely in the wrestling area and
the head cannot be touching the protection area.

Wrestlers can also win by technical superiority, meaning they have
earned 10 more points than their opponent. Once a wrestler has a 10-

point lead, wait for a neutral position on the mat and then stop the bout, asking him if he wants to continue. Don't interrupt the bout until action is completed. As mentioned before, in some cases the winner isn't given the choice to continue; the bout is over once a wrestler achieves technical superiority.

These last three chapters should provide you with a solid foundation for refereeing Greco-Roman and freestyle wrestling. However, be sure to work closely with the appropriate sanctioning body and obtain the complete rules and regulations for whatever competition you are preparing to officiate. Refereeing, whether for folkstyle or any of the three styles addressed in these final chapters, is a gratifying endeavor, and it is vital to the sport. Keep up with the rules, sharpen your mechanics and referee to the best of your ability!

NFHS Officiating Wrestling Signals

1. Starting the match

2. Stopping the match

3. Time-out

4. Start injury clock

5. Start blood clock

6. Stop blood/injury clock

7. Neutral position

8. No control

9. Out of bounds

10. Wrestler in control (right or left hand)

11. Defer choice

12. Potentially dangerous
(right or left hand)

13. Stalemate

14. Caution—false start or incorrect
starting procedure

15. Stalling (right or left hand)

16. Interlocking hands or grasping clothing

17. Reversal

18. Technical violation

19. Illegal hold or unnecessary roughness

20. Near fall

21. Awarding points (right or left hand)

22. Unsportsmanlike conduct
(right or left hand)

23. Flagrant misconduct
(right or left hand)

24. Coach misconduct
(right or left hand)

GLOSSARY

Folkstyle Wrestling Terms

advantage—A wrestler is in a position of advantage when he is in control and maintaining restraining power over his opponent. Control is the determining factor.

bridge—A wrestler creates a bridge to support himself on his head, elbows and feet to keep from touching his shoulders to the mat.

bye—A wrestler receives a bye to move on to the next round of a tournament when he has no opponent in a given round. A bye is allowed for the first round only; thereafter it is considered a forfeit.

caution—Penalty that can be issued for assuming an incorrect starting position or a false start.

countermove—Move that stops or blocks an opponent's attack. Wrestlers may score on a countermove.

decision—Victory by points, where the winner's score exceeds the loser's by seven points or less (nine points or less in international matches).

default—A default is awarded when one of the competitors is unable to continue for any reason.

defensive starting position—The defensive wrestler's starting position, which requires the wrestler to be at the center of the circle on the heels of his hands and on his knees, with the knees behind and parallel to the rear starting line.

disqualification—Wrestlers are disqualified on the first offense for any act which the referee considers serious enough to remove the offender from the premises. Wrestlers may also be disqualified from a match in progress on the fourth penalty for cumulative violations including: illegal holds, technical violations, stalling and unsportsmanlike conduct.

escape—When a defensive wrestler gains a neutral position and the opponent has lost control, an escape is earned.

fall—When a wrestler pins his opponent's shoulders or scapulas to the mat for two seconds. Both shoulders or scapulas must be in continuous contact with the mat during those two seconds.

folkstyle—The style used in U.S. high schools and colleges; includes holds above and below the waist.

forfeit—When a wrestler for any reason fails to report for a match.

illegal hold—Holds are illegal when a body part is forced beyond the limit of normal range of motion.

inbounds—Wrestlers are inbounds if the supporting parts of either wrestler are touching or within the boundary lines.

injury time—When wrestlers are injured, they are allowed one and a half total minutes of injury time in one bout.

major decision—Decision where the winner's total is 8 to 14 points greater than his opponent.

mat area—The mat area includes the wrestling mat and a space of at least 10 feet (3 meters) surrounding the mat, as well as the team benches and scorer's table, where facilities permit.

near fall—When any part of both shoulders or scapulas of the defensive wrestler is held within four inches or less of the mat. It is also awarded when one shoulder or scapula of the defensive wrestler is touching the mat and the other shoulder or scapula is at an angle of 45 degrees or less to the mat, or when the defensive wrestler is held in a high bridge on both elbows.

neutral starting position—Starting position that requires both wrestlers to be stationary and opposite each other with one foot on the green or red area of the starting lines and the other foot on the line or the line extended, or behind the foot on the line with no part of the body touching the mat in front of the lead foot.

offensive starting position—Offensive wrestler's starting position, which is at the right or left side of the opponent with at least one knee on the mat on the near side of the opponent. The offensive wrestler places the palm of one hand on or over the back of the defensive wrestler's elbow; he places the other arm loosely around the defensive wrestler's body.

optional offensive starting position—The offensive wrestler may position himself on either side or to the rear of his opponent, supporting his weight on both feet, one knee or both knees. His hands are on his opponent's back with thumbs touching; only his hands are in contact with the defensive wrestler.

out of bounds—Out of bounds occurs when a supporting point of both wrestlers is on or beyond the boundary line.

reversal—When a wrestler comes out from underneath the other wrestler and gains control of his opponent on the mat or in a rear standing position while the supporting parts of either wrestler are inbounds; worth two points.

slam—When a wrestler lifts and returns an opponent to the mat with unnecessary force. A slam is illegal.

stalemate—When the wrestlers are interlocked in a position, other than a pinning situation, in which neither wrestler can improve his position, or when either wrestler locks his hands around one leg of the opponent to prevent scoring.

stalling—When a wrestler fails to make an honest attempt to wrestle aggressively regardless of position or the time or score of the match.

supporting points—The parts of the body touching the mat that bear the wrestlers' weight. When wrestlers are down on the mat, the usual points of support are: knees, buttocks, hands or side of the thigh.

takedown—When a wrestler in a neutral position gains control over his opponent down on the mat while the supporting parts of either wrestler are inbounds; worth two points.

technical fall—When a wrestler wins by 15 or more points.

technical violations—These include, but are not limited to, assuming an incorrect starting position, making a false start, intentionally going out of the wrestling area, interlocking or overlapping hands around the opponent's body and grasping clothing or ear guards. A wrestler is penalized one point for each of his first two violations, two points for the third violation and is disqualified for the fourth.

unnecessary roughness—Physical acts that go beyond normal aggressiveness (e.g., a forceful trip, using the forearm or elbow in a punishing way).

unsporting conduct—Physical or nonphysical acts before, during or after a match that show poor sportsmanship (e.g., failing to comply with a referee's direction, taunting, spitting, swearing).

wrestling area—Circular area on the mat that is a minimum of 28 feet (8.5 meters) in diameter. It is surrounded by a safety mat about 5 feet (1.5 meters) wide.

Greco-Roman and Freestyle Wrestling Terms

amplitude—A throw in which the opponent is lifted above the attacking wrestler's waist.

body lock—When a wrestler locks his hands around the opponent's body to execute a throw.

brutality—Unnecessary roughness with the intent to injure the opponent. This results in automatic disqualification.

central wrestling area—The middle of the mat, seven meters across in national and international competitions, where the wrestling should take place.

correct hold—A well-executed throw. Points can be awarded for a correct hold without the hold resulting in a takedown or putting the opponent in danger.

exposure—When the defensive wrestler's back is turned toward the mat and the head or an elbow is not touching the mat.

fleeing a hold—When a wrestler avoids his opponent's attack and is penalized by one or two points depending on whether the hold was fled from a danger position (two points).

freestyle—One of two international wrestling styles. Use of legs is permitted.

grand amplitude—High, sweeping throw in which the opponent is lifted entirely off the mat.

Greco-Roman—One of two international wrestling styles. A wrestler cannot attack his opponent's legs or use his own legs in an attack.

gut wrench—When a wrestler uses his opponent's torso and turns him to score points.

instantaneous fall—When both shoulders touch the mat but not long enough for a fall. Two points are awarded to the opponent.

overtime—When the score is tied at the end of regulation or when the leading scorer has not scored at least three technical points.

paddles—Red, white and blue paddles used by the judge and the mat chairman to indicate their decisions.

par terre—Means "on the ground." The defensive wrestler will have three supporting points in contact with the mat; one is with the knee.

passivity—Stalling and avoiding wrestling. This is penalized with a warning and the passive wrestler is placed in the underneath par terre position.

passivity zone—Band one meter wide inside the edge of the mat. When wrestlers are in this zone, the referee yells "Zone!" and the wrestlers attempt to move back to the center of the mat.

total wrestling—Concept that both wrestlers must be aggressive and active at all times.

INDEX

ABOUT THE AUTHOR

Officiating Wrestling was written by the American Sport Education Program (ASEP) in cooperation with the National Federation of State High School Associations (NFHS). Based in Indianapolis, the NFHS is the rules authority for high school sports in the United States. Hundreds of thousands of officials nationwide and worldwide rely on the NFHS for officiating guidance. ASEP is a division of Human Kinetics, Inc., based in Champaign, Illinois, and has been a world leader in providing educational courses and resources to professional and volunteer coaches, officials, parents and sport administrators for more than 20 years. ASEP and the NFHS have teamed up to offer books, CDs and online courses for high school officials through the NFHS Officials Education Program.

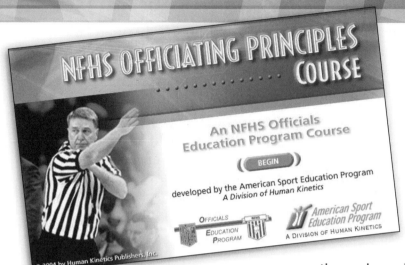